TO

_____

FROM

_____

DATE

_____

DARE TO BUILD A LIFE YOU LOVE

GROWING BOLDLY

EMILY LEY

THOMAS NELSON
Since 1798

Published in Nashville, Tennessee, by Thomas Nelson. Thomas Nelson is a registered trademark of HarperCollins Christian Publishing, Inc.

Published in association with Folio Literary Management LLC, 630 Ninth Avenue, Suite 1101, New York, New York 10036.

Thomas Nelson titles may be purchased in bulk for educational, business, fund-raising, or sales promotional use. For information, please email SpecialMarkets@ ThomasNelson.com.

Unless otherwise noted, Scripture quotations are taken from the Holy Bible, New International Version®, NIV®. Copyright © 1973, 1978, 1984, 2011 by Biblica, Inc.® Used by permission of Zondervan. All rights reserved worldwide. www.Zondervan.com. The "NIV" and "New International Version" are trademarks registered in the United States Patent and Trademark Office by Biblica, Inc.®

Scripture quotations marked NKJV are from the New King James Version®. © 1982 by Thomas Nelson. Used by permission. All rights reserved.

ISBN 978-1-4002-1133-3 (eBook)
ISBN 978-1-4002-1131-9 (HC)
ISBN 978-1404-11547-7 (custom)
ISBN 978-1-4002-2548-5 (audio)

Printed in China

21 22 23 24 25 DSC 10 9 8 7 6 5 4 3 2 1

To Tyler:

You are good as gold, my precious boy.
Dare to build a life you love.
I'll be here cheering you on.

And to Team Simplified:

I could not write these words without you.
You exemplify what this book is about.

CONTENTS

Introduction   **vii**

B: BELIEVE IN WHO YOU ARE, AND WHOSE YOU ARE
    1. Call Out the Lies and Face the Fears   **5**
    2. Get to Know the Real You   **19**
    3. Get Comfortable with Confidence   **47**

U: UTILIZE WHAT YOU HAVE
    4. Dig Up Your Grit   **57**
    5. Stand Strong on Your Story   **69**
    6. Raise Your Average   **79**

I: IMAGINE THE LIFE YOU DREAM OF
    7. Claim Your Calling   **89**
    8. Design Your Road Map   **103**

L: LOVE PEOPLE WELL
    9. Lead With Integrity and Passion   **123**
    10. Serve With Kindness   **137**
    11. Choose Legacy   **147**

D: DO WHAT MATTERS. FORGET THE REST
    12. Fight Like an Underdog   **163**
    13. Pursue What Makes You Come Alive   **175**
    14. Dig In   **187**

Chase Your Rainbow   **197**
Acknowledgments   **200**
Notes   **201**

INTRODUCTION

H i, friends.

Let's kick this book off with a gut check. How are you? Like, how are you *really*?

I finished writing this book just one month before COVID-19 swept our world. Little did I know what our lives would look like in the months following my submission of this manuscript. Like the lives of people across America and worldwide, *everything* in my life was turned upside down. Suddenly, I became a homeschooling mom navigating an uncertain future amid a terrifying global pandemic. The landscape of business changed. Our global economy took an enormous hit. And I found myself struggling to answer three small children's seemingly unanswerable questions about life and death.

And yet this experience has been life-changing in our house in beautiful ways. Quarantine magically, devastatingly cleared our schedules and we suddenly found ourselves appreciating the small things once again (time together, fresh food to eat, and joy found at home when the hustle of life comes to a screeching halt). Like the canals in Italy, whose once-murky waters cleared from lack of boats and pollution, our priorities crystallized. And as the weeks and months stretched on, I found myself both grateful for the lessons learned and hopeful for brighter, happier, more meaningful days to come. In short, the challenges of 2020 taught me a lot.

This book is written with love and hope and is centered on truths that are unchanging. Life is short. You are worthy. And it's entirely possible to bloom in the driest of seasons, to flourish when life feels as if it's falling apart.

Even if your heart has been ravaged by grief, fear, or uncertainty, my hope is that the words in this book help you evaluate where you are, determine where you'd like to be, and map out a solid plan for how you're going to get there. Let's get to work.

•   •   •

Twelve years ago, I founded Simplified, a brand of day planners and organizational tools, to help women simplify their lives— and to solve problems I was facing in my own. Through a lot of ups and downs, I've taken Simplified from a solo side hustle in my guest room to a multimillion-dollar company with nine team members and more than 150 products in our online shop, plus licensed collections in Walmart, Target, Office Depot, and Staples. Sometimes I pinch myself when I look at how far we've come, as if it happened by some stroke of luck. But really, this dream became my reality because I decided there had to be something better than where I was and dug up the courage to do the work—to boldly build a career, a family, and a life I loved.

I identified a quirk about myself (a gift, even), allowed that quirk to develop into a passion, and created a life out of it. I created Simplified and the Simplified Planner because I live a real life. It's messy and complicated and sometimes really un-simplified *because that's life*. But God gave me an ability to see to the heart of mess and complication and to—when possible—sort through it methodically and precisely, to apply routine and structure, and to make something peaceful out of something otherwise frenetic. My hope is that my words here help you do exactly that, as you look at your own growth and goals.

I've grown a lot over the last twelve years. But growing is one thing. We all do it every day, whether we like it or not. Growing *boldly* (especially during seasons of uncertainty) is another thing entirely. Merriam-Webster defines "bold" as "showing an ability to take risks; confident and courageous." In the pages that follow, I'm going to invite you to challenge the idea that where you are today is as good as it gets. Together we're going to push our boundaries, challenge what we "think we know" about ourselves, strip the layers of doubt and fear, and allow ourselves to be inspired by stories of other coura-geous women owning their imperfect journeys and building lives they love—even in the face of unprecedented hardships and tragedy.

Growing boldly often looks a lot like allowing your outsides to match your insides—your words to match your thoughts and your actions to match your beliefs. Do you ever feel the dis-connect? The distance between who you are at your very core and the way you're living at home, at work, or in your circle of friends? Bridging the gap takes work, but mostly it requires courage—the courage to own what you want and the confidence to go out on a limb despite the fear of criticism or failure.

As an almost thirty-eight-year-old woman whose outsides are more reflective of her insides than ever before, let me tell you—it feels good. I'm inviting you to bridge your own gap: to be authentically, imperfectly, confidently you—in every way—as we embark on this journey together.

We all come from different places and have different obstacles in becoming who we want to be. But one thing remains: you have more control than you think, and you get to make choices. God has given you what you need. He's set you in front of two paths. One looks exactly like the road you're on. The other is a little more obscured, a little difficult to peer down very far. But you know the very best version of you might be down that road. The life you will unapologetically claim as your own (in the next section!) is on the other side of the lies you're consuming and the fear you're buried beneath.

> You have more control than you think, and you get to make choices.

So how do we get where we want to go? We take a step. We work. We make a call, send an email, say no to whatever we can't commit to right now and yes to the thing that scares us most. We take brave steps forward, even if we're scared.

Forward momentum requires *movement*. And hard work sometimes means we have to break a sweat.

Never be afraid of getting sweaty.

Of staying up late.

Of figuring out how to do what you don't know by googling and asking and trying a hundred times until you nail it.

I will always value *heart over hustle* and I sincerely believe there is a time and a season for everything, "a time to plant and a time to uproot . . . a time to tear down and a time to build" (Ecclesiastes 3:2–3). But I also know that I won't become who I want to be if I'm not willing to get in the arena and fight for it. Nobody ever achieved anything or transformed by sitting on the couch and propelling through a Netflix series.

> Forward momentum requires *movement*. And hard work sometimes means we have to break a sweat.

You can break free from the chains that keep you on that couch by doing work: uncovering the lies the world, the media, and your Instagram feed have told you about yourself. Dismantling the unrealistic, unreachable standard of perfection you've solidified in your head. Discovering what it is you want to do and who it is you want to become. And telling the fear that's holding you back that *it's your turn now*, and it's time for him to take a backseat.

IT STARTS WITH A SPARK

On a car ride back from Christmas in Pensacola with our families, as fresh newlyweds, I told my husband, Bryan, that I was miserable in my career. I'd earned a master's degree, climbed the corporate ladder, and was helping run a Women in Leadership and Philanthropy program at a large state university. The female alumni who were members of our organization were incredible. They were making big things happen in business, were pushing social issues forward, and were doing amazing things for our community.

But the environment was stifling, and I felt like I was suffocating. I longed for the freedom to go out and *do*—like the community women who were part of our organization. More than anything I just wanted *freedom* to be, do, see, create, and make a bigger impact. I wanted to spread my wings and do work that made me excited. Eventually I wanted a family, and I kept thinking about how I wouldn't be able to chaperone field trips or even make it to school performances in my current situation, working long hours.

I kept coming back to this quote: "Try to learn to breathe deeply, really to taste food when you eat, and when you sleep, really to sleep. Try as much as possible to be wholly alive with all your might, and when you laugh, laugh like hell. And when you get angry, get good and angry. Try to be *alive*."[1]

I was not alive. I didn't know what to do, but I had to find a way to become alive again.

Though they felt few and far between, I started to iden-tify the parts of my current job that made me happy—creating fliers for events, designing logos for different programs, and—oddly—writing thoughtful thank-you notes to our donors. My fascination with design and writing began to grow. On a whim, I told Bryan I wanted to make notecards and sell them on Etsy (I'd always loved stationery and paper goods but could never afford the fancy kind). Etsy was a new platform at that time, where makers could sell their creations. The only problem was, I didn't know how to use Etsy or make notecards. And I didn't have a company name, business license, resale certificate, or well, any money. We were Dave Ramsey–ing our way through student-loan and credit card debt, and my weekly envelopes had little to spare for a new hobby. But I felt a little spark, and I followed it.

First things first: How do I get a business license? Googles "how to get a business license in Florida."

Ugh, I need a name. Emily Ley Paper.

Finds the website. Files the paperwork online. Business license in hand in only a few minutes.

The rush of figuring out something I had no clue how to do was exciting. So I did it again.

Can I use what I have on my old home PC (Microsoft Publisher, Word, and Excel) to make notecards since I can't afford fancy software that I'm not even sure the name of? Yes!

How the heck do I do that? Googles "How to use Microsoft Publisher." Reads articles about what a terrible program

Publisher is for graphic designers. *Good thing I'm not actually a graphic designer and can't afford anything beyond what I have.* So I just dove in.

Within days, I had used cardstock leftover from DIY wedding projects to create folded note cards, matched them with envelopes I had on hand and ribbon from my gift-wrap stash. Add in my top-notch Googling skills, watching every free YouTube video out there, and my own insatiable desire to create something of my own outside the corporate workplace I was in every day, which felt so square-peg-in-a-round-hole, and there was no stopping me.

Let me be clear: this is *more* than just a book about how to leave your job to start a business. If that's your calling, go for it! It was mine at that time. But that doesn't have to be your calling. This book is about building a life that honors what gives *you* life—a life that gives back to you, that nourishes you, and that causes you to thrive, whether you make money at it or not. There is nothing wrong with having a job that pays the bills and a separate passion or calling that inspires your life. It's all connected.

I spent more than two years selling as many notecards as I could, putting every dollar I earned back into my fledgling business in the hopes of one day being able to take a paycheck. I'd work late into the evenings, after my day job, creating my logo, learning how to build a free website, and navigating the new worlds of Twitter and Facebook. I'd spend five hours on something, realize I had done it all wrong, and have to start at square one. I can't even begin to tell you how many times that happened. Some nights I'd get so excited about a project or a new skill I was trying to figure out that I'd lose all sense of time and look up to see the sun peeking through the blinds of our guest room.

A SEASON FOR EVERYTHING

For a season, I worked like mad. And the business grew—fast—because I was willing to put in the work needed to achieve my goals. Now, let it be known, I'm a workhorse. Putting in the work has never been my problem. My problem has been acknowledging that hustle should only last for a season. We weren't made to go ninety miles an hour nonstop. A marathon runner has to pace herself to catch her breath. A race car driver has to pull in for pitstops. A mountain climber has to find a spot to lay down her gear, eat and drink something, and rest her body.

In Ecclesiastes 3, we see that for every action—to work, to be born, to build, to plant—there is a balancing force found right next to it—to rest, to die, to tear down, to harvest. Without this balance, things get wonky. And we burn out.

No, *wonky* isn't in the Bible. But you know what I mean. If we trust God and believe there is a time and a season for everything, we have to honor both the times of hard work and sweat, as well as the seasons of rest and refueling. It's the same reason we grieve instead of laughing amid a loss. Or harvest in the fall instead of planting. Some of these seasons make

TO EVERYTHING

THERE IS A SEASON

AND A TIME

FOR EVERY PURPOSE

UNDER HEAVEN.

—*Ecclesiastes 3:1* NKJV

perfect sense—even if we don't enjoy them. But some of them are difficult to honor.

This has been the hardest lesson for me as my business has grown and as I've learned more about effort, energy, and the entrepreneurial spirit. I have to know when to set down my gear and stop climbing the mountain—in work and in life—not for forever, because seasons change, but for a while, until my strength is renewed, my spirit is reenergized, and my boldness has been recharged.

Then I can get back to work.

Whatever season you're in, I know we can discover together what will lead you to the fuel you need to build something beautiful.

BUILDING IN ACTION

So, like Mary Oliver said, what will you "do with your one wild and precious life?"[2] You only get one shot at this. And your time has come.

Though you might not have a perfectly laid-out ten-year plan, five-year plan, or even one-month plan, you are building a life with every decision, every choice—big, small, or tiny—you make. You're creating a legacy that will live on long past you. The question I want you to ask yourself is this: *Am I building a life I love?*

You are the author of the book of your life. Only you can build a life you love. God has given you gifts, talents, and skills to use in *His kingdom work* and is calling you to do *something* with your time here. Throughout this book, I will walk you through my own sometimes-crazy and imperfect adventure to discovering my calling and rediscovering it as things have changed and shifted from season to season.

I believe there are five key practices to building a life you love.

> You are building a life with every decision, every choice—big, small, or tiny—you make.

B: Believe in Who You Are (and Whose You Are)
Figure out what makes you tick. Own it confidently.

U: Use What You Have
Gather all your grit, learned lessons, supporters, and tools. Discount nothing.

I: Imagine the Life You Dream Of
Decide what you want to make happen and make a plan for it.

L: Love Your People (and All People) Well
Be a good human. Create legacy, not work. Contribute positively to the kingdom.

D: Do What Matters; Forget the Rest
Clear the clutter. Cultivate clarity. Do hard work, and don't forget to feed your soul.

Building a life you love requires action. Sometimes this looks like hustle and hard work, sweat and late nights. Sometimes this looks like rest and reflection, stilling our hands and quieting our hearts to tune in to God's whisperings in our life, allowing Him to refuel our souls.

Many books have been written to tell you that you are a "boss babe," that you can achieve #allthethings all at once, and that it's okay to hustle till it hurts. If you're looking for a generic "go, girl" kick in the pants, this book isn't for you. If you're looking for a friend who has built something from nothing by going brave, trusting her gut, working really, really hard, and . . . well, also making a million mistakes, then this book is for you. I'm going to push you to think outside the box, to question *everything*, and to take action toward what you want.

In the pages that follow, I want to call your attention to the special way this book has been laid out. I believe it's essential to dig deep into the heart of so many important concepts and stories as part of the BUILD philosophy and then connect those ideas back to truths found elsewhere—in the Bible, from other insightful writers, and even in poetry. You'll find a short snippet of inspiration at the end of each chapter, followed by a blessing—or benediction. My hope is that as you think on the ideas and principles that preceded, this handful of questions for you to consider as you apply the concepts to your own life will spur you to action.

I'm so glad you're here. Don't ever doubt that you have a seat at the table. You belong even before you *believe* you

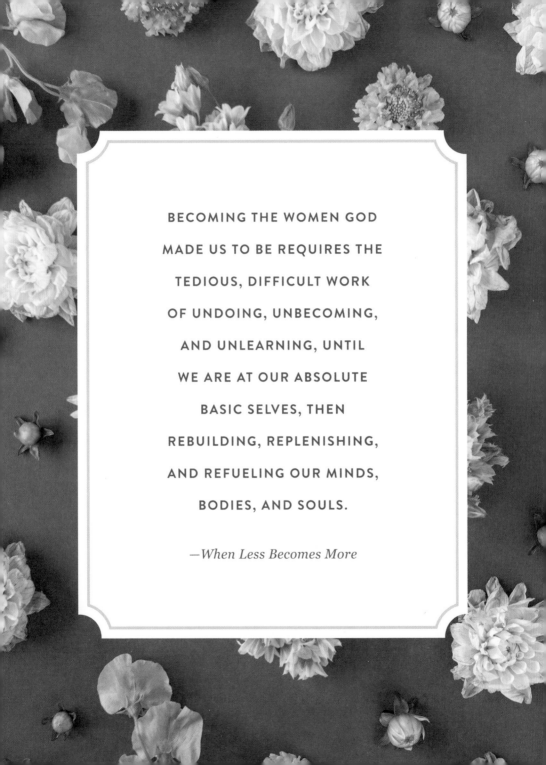

BECOMING THE WOMEN GOD
MADE US TO BE REQUIRES THE
TEDIOUS, DIFFICULT WORK
OF UNDOING, UNBECOMING,
AND UNLEARNING, UNTIL
WE ARE AT OUR ABSOLUTE
BASIC SELVES, THEN
REBUILDING, REPLENISHING,
AND REFUELING OUR MINDS,
BODIES, AND SOULS.

—*When Less Becomes More*

> You have the right and the power to build a life you love—one that is whole, meaningful, and authentically yours.

belong. You have the right and the power to build a life you love—one that is whole, meaningful, and authentically yours. You have the power to propel that business. To cultivate your home. To grow your family. To release that vice. To make that change. To create that book or art or recipe or ministry. To come back. To rebuild. To thrive.

You also have the power to blame circumstance for your stagnation. To give up when things get too real or too frightening. You can let all those things keep you stuck on the couch. The choice is yours.

You can build a life you love . . . if you dare to do the work.

xo,

Emily

benediction

The Lord bless you

and keep you;

the Lord make his face shine on you

and be gracious to you;

the Lord turn his face toward you

and give you peace.

—Numbers 6:24-26

BUILD

*Believe in who you are,
and whose you are.*

Part One

I wrote the words on the previous page in my last book, during a time when I felt very stuck and unsure about the path forward, but certain I had work to do. If you are feeling stuck right now, I want you to know that's a perfectly okay place to be. Before we start moving forward, let's explore where we are. To discover the strength and spirit within ourselves, we have to get to the core of who we are. At your core is where the most authentic version of yourself is buried—beneath piles of unrealistic standards and lies about who we are and who we are not. You're not perfect. Neither am I. It's time to get to know who you really are: your beautiful quirks, your unique interests, and the beliefs and values you stand for.

1

CALL OUT THE LIES
AND FACE THE FEARS

*Can you remember who you were before the
world told you who you should become?*

CHARLES BUKOWSKI

To believe unapologetically and wholeheartedly in who you are, you have to know the girl we're talking about. You have to get to know you—the real you—the one buried deep down. And to get to her, we have to dig her out. Strip away the lies and untruths and fears you've been barricading yourself behind so that you can truly blossom. Some are obvious, some not so much.

Some lies are so subtle yet so powerful that they're like tiny chains attached to our ankles, holding us back from taking that next right step forward. And yet they've been there so long that we don't even feel their grip, the bruises, the indentations they've left. Look at your wrists, your ankles. What chains, big or small, are attached there? Let's work together to name them. To call them out and strip away whatever power they have over you. The key to the lock on those chains? It's in your heart and in your words. When you identify the lies you've been telling yourself about who you are—out loud, you turn the key, release the lock, and step out of their stronghold.

Let's be clear. The Enemy—and the world—love to tell you who you are not.

You're not skinny enough.

You're not smart enough.

You're not a good enough mom.

You're not crafty enough, educated enough, or wealthy enough.

You can't reach that goal because it's too hard.

You can't dream that dream because you don't deserve it.

You're not worthy of that kind of love because of your past.

Says who? Some stranger on the internet? The media? Your coworkers? The other moms at school?

Jessa, who painted the cover for this book, calls these false stories "mess." I call them "noise." Whatever you call it, turn that garbage down. *Mess* might be a better word though. Jessa says that when she hears her grandma refer to something as "mess" (like, "Clean that mess up!"), she knows Grandma means business.

So here I am telling you to *turn that mess down*. And I mean business.

Release yourself from the lies so you can fully see (and then believe in!) who you are.

You know what you're *not*? You're not helpless. You're not hopeless. You're not too old, too young, or too inexperienced.

You're not the sum of your doubts. You're not too far gone. You're not too deep in the hole. You're not your childhood. You're not that mistake you made. You're not that thing that happened to you.

Struggle is where we are made strong.

You are spirited, strong, and bold. You're growing every minute of every day. Why not grow boldly?

FAITH IN PROGRESS

One of the biggest false narratives I struggle with is that I'm ill-equipped to write about matters of faith. I've got a whole album of lies playing on repeat in my head *right this minute*, as I type these words. I wasn't raised going to church every Sunday, I didn't study theology, and I have *a lot* of questions. I feel as if I'm not worthy to talk about such complex and important matters for fear that I'll get something wrong or that someone will find me out—that I'm just a girl who loves God and is trying her best to learn more about Him and live life well. But I'm leaning in and peeling away that lie, and God is using that freedom to teach me more and make me more confident in who He is and who I am.

You know that false narrative, right? That you need to have all the answers (and all your ducks in a row) in order to take the first step or even talk about something that matters to you? Maybe you've experienced something similar in other areas of your life. Perhaps the lie that tells you not to pursue building that brand because you're not interesting enough. Or the lie that you'll always be overweight because you're not powerful enough to overcome temptation? Or the one that says you have to stay at that job that sucks the life out of you because no other company will want you? What about the lie that your marriage is too messy to ever be fully healed? That you don't deserve happiness because the choices you made in the past are too much for God? Or what about the lie that you're not a good mom because you sometimes feed your kids SpaghettiOs and your laundry piles up and you lose your patience with them?

What about the lie that you don't have enough energy, enough money, enough support, enough time, or enough education to do all the things?

Editing and revising this book in the middle of a global pandemic, I can tell you this: it's never been more critical to kick the lies to the curb. There are times in life when we must do this work so that we can make great change in our lives. And there are times when we must do this work so that we have truths upon which to stand in the middle of the storm. No matter the season or circumstance, we have to peel back the lies to unveil the truth.

WHAT I KNOW

Throughout this book, we're going to talk about the things we know for sure. Now, listen. I don't know many things for sure.

But I know a few things *for sure.* And I'm always adding to the list. No seriously, I keep a list in a Google Doc. It's an awesome place to visit when you're having a bad day because the words on that page are indisputable. Want to make your own? It's easy! Just open a new Google Doc (or maybe even utilize the notes app on your phone), and start your list.

And here is what I know right now: God is calling me to be bold. In my life and in this book. Bold about faith,

> The best way to not feel hopeless is to get up and do something. Don't wait for good things to happen to you. If you go out and make some good things happen, you will fill the world with hope. You'll fill yourself with hope.
>
> BARACK OBAMA

about business, about things I've mastered, things I don't want to face, things I'm still learning, things I've failed at, and things I may never figure out—all while feeling the accompanying discomfort and facing all the fears. He's calling me to step into my own unique identity—and I know He's calling you too.

PUT FEAR IN ITS PLACE

Sometimes we believe lies about ourselves because they touch a nerve. They connect to deep-seated fears. Yes, sometimes

Things I know *for sure*

The sun will come up tomorrow. God never forgets. He brings it up every single morning with the same energy and enthusiasm He had on that very first day.

God's love for us isn't bound by time, space, or mistakes.

Family comes first. Full stop.

_____

_____

_____

_____

_____

_____

_____

_____

_____

_____

_____

_____

those fears are surface level (*Will I look dumb? Will people laugh at me?*), but sometimes they're deep and dark and all too real (*What if the worst happens and I can't go on?*).

Among my greatest, deepest, darkest fears is concern for my kids' health and safety—a fear that's been made even more real during the time of COVID-19. When I think of friends who have met this deepest and darkest of fears, I think of Christi.

Christi and I met in college thanks to mutual friends. She is tall, blond, bursting with a warm Southern personality, and was valedictorian of her graduating class. She was the envy of many, to be sure. And Christi has a heart of gold. She married her husband, Justin, after college graduation, and they planned to have children soon after. Sadly, they were met with miscarriage, after miscarriage, after miscarriage. But after a few years, Christi gave birth to their oldest daughter, Charleigh. And, shortly after, a son, Braden. It seemed like a happy ending to a hard season filled with loss. Until Christi met her biggest fear head on.

After expressing a few concerns to their pediatrician and visiting a couple doctors, Christi and Justin landed in a neurologist's office with their son, Braden, where he was diagnosed with a rare genetic disease called cystinosis. Only five hundred people in the United States have the disease, and there is little funding for treatment or a cure. In fact, the neurologist had never seen a case in his years of practice. The bad news continued. Cystinosis, he explained, is terminal.

That doctor's appointment was eight years ago. Braden is a thriving, confident, energetic eight-year-old. He takes medications daily and visits a specialist every three months. He is also the proud older brother to Dax, who was also diagnosed with cystinosis. If you're counting, that's three adorable kids. And they recently added Karagan, another daughter, to the family.

I've always had a special place in my heart for Christi's boys, for her journey as a mom, and for their family in general. My company does an annual fundraiser for the Cystinosis Research Foundation in honor of Christi's boys, but I've never sat down with Christi to break down, in depth, *how in the world* she carries on with life so joyfully and so faithfully in the face of this monumental fear. When I texted her to ask if she'd allow me to interview her to share her story in this book, she responded with a resounding YES!

"Our glory story can't bring glory to God if we're not sharing it with everyone!" she said.

Let's just count that as one of many times I was struck and deeply moved by Christi's wholehearted words. And she means it. Some of the things Christi said may surprise you. You may wonder if she *really* believes what she says. One thing's for sure: she does. To know Christi is to know her sincere heart. And to have a conversation with her is to see the fire in her eyes and feel beneath her words a fierce belief in the King of all kings. When we talk, I'm always captivated by her words, trying to draw out every nugget of truth and goodness from her conviction.

What's your glory story?

_____

_____

_____

_____

_____

_____

_____

_____

What do you want it to communicate to the world?

_____

_____

_____

_____

_____

_____

_____

_____

_____

When Christi and I sat down together, I asked about her boys and how they're doing.

"The kid is confident." She laughs as she tells me about Braden's recent basketball game. "He told me he was going to play a joke on everyone. I asked, 'What do you mean, buddy? Like, a practical joke?' He said, 'No, Mom. Like I'm going to walk in and people are going to think, *Man, he's small. I bet he's not very good.* And then I'm just gonna be *so* good! It'll be so funny!'"

I laughed so hard! Of course he said that. She told me Braden has low muscle tone and is a good foot or two shorter than everyone else because of cystinosis. He takes medications and receives shots daily. And then he's off to play golf. Or basketball. Or dominate everyone at something else, the only way he knows how.

I love this kid.

I dove right in with my questions, asking Christi how in the world she gets up every morning, puts her feet on the floor, and manages life as a mom to four kids, two of whom have this terrible disease.

She laughed hard. "I just do it. I don't have a choice. And I remind myself that if something is out of my control in every way possible, then it must be God's will for my life."

I didn't even know what to say to this. What bold conviction.

As a believer long before her boys' diagnosis, Christi has always wanted her life and work to bring glory to God. "God gave our family a chance to do exactly that. Life is not about healthy children. And we do hard things."

I caught onto that last phrase, one that I'd heard her share before. It's the mantra of their family: We do hard things.

When Christi and Justin tuck their kids into bed at night, they ask them four things:

1. What was the best part of your day?
2. What was one thing you did *just* to make someone else happy today?
3. What is one thing you can do better tomorrow?
4. What was one hard thing you did today?

After each child shares his or her answer to the last question, navigating the sibling disagreement or overcoming the playground altercation or conquering the fear they had standing up in front of their class, Christi says, "We do hard things."

They put fear in its place. And it has stuck.

This phrase is an example of something I greatly admire about Christi's parenting. They speak certain words over their children routinely to help shape their kids' future self-talk. Think about that. The words we repeatedly tell ourselves—and our children—become the voice inside. I just love how Christi and Justin intentionally fill their children with *truths* about God and *truths* about themselves. What a beautiful way to combat the lies and false narratives early on.

When her boys encounter the difficulties their disease presents as it progresses, they'll remember: we do hard things. When her daughters witness their brothers' suffering, they'll remember: we do hard things. When life throws whatever curveballs at her kids, they'll remember: we do hard things. They'll also remember: *This is where God meets me, in the hard stuff. And I am not defined by the hard thing but by the One who walks me through it.*

Christi's older daughter often has deep anxieties and questions about her brothers' struggles. I asked how Christi helps her navigate those fears, and she said she points it all back to Jesus. Jesus was God's own Son, and even He was not free from suffering.

Everyone suffers—some suffer with finances, some with addiction, some with loss, some with broken relationships, some with incurable diseases. "This is our story," Christi explains. "Our glory story. And we'll continue to use our lives, just as we did before our boys were diagnosed, to point people back to the Lord."

I asked if Christi prays for a cure (a few very hopeful medical advancements are being made in the quest for a cure for this rare disease thanks to a few passionate parents and supporters). She said, "Of course. I pray for a cure—or something greater."

Disbelief rose up in me. "What on earth could be greater?"

"If God is who He says He is, if I believe what I say I believe, then there could be something greater than a cure. I read in *The Red Sea Rules*, 'Be more concerned for God's glory than for your relief.'"[3]

This was the mic-drop moment that made me repeat silently inside my head: *Have mercy on me, God, and my disbelief.*

Christi has found a strength I cannot comprehend. A strength that has been hard-won and that she has *chosen* by calling upon the truths she knows about God to embolden her faith and put fear in its place. I'm not sure I've witnessed such spirit, strength, and boldness in a long time. Our conversation moved me to identify my own unspoken fears, to name them, and to feel confident in my own glory story—whether the outcome makes sense to me or the world. God makes no mistakes. Put your fears in their place so you can grow in the way the world needs you to—boldly and beautifully.

I hope Christi's story inspired you in the ways it touched me. If you'd like to learn more about cystinosis, visit CystinosisResearch.org.

benediction

May you have the courage to believe in God's truths over your lies.

To hold within you the unwavering knowledge that because of and

despite your circumstances, you have the power to take the next

small step toward who you want to become. By birthright, you have

everything you need, planted deep within you by God Himself. May you

unearth it without hesitation. I hope Christi's story inspired you in the

ways it touched me. If you'd like to learn more about Cystinosis,

visit CystinosisResearch.org.

reflection

What lies about yourself are playing on repeat in your head?

What false narratives are others telling you about who you are?

Christi's family does hard things. What hard things does your family do?

What hard things do you do individually?

How has fear played a role in the way you've held yourself back?

There is boldness born in facing fears and lies—

glory stories being written in each of us.

What is your glory story?

2

GET TO KNOW
THE REAL YOU

*You become. It takes a long time. That's why it doesn't happen
often to people who break easily, or have sharp edges, or who
have been carefully kept. Generally by the time you are Real,
most of your hair has been loved off, and your eyes drop out and
you get loose in the joints and very shabby. But these things don't
matter at all, because once you are Real you can't be ugly.*

MARJORY WILLIAMS BIANCO, *THE VELVETEEN RABBIT*

You may be thinking, *Fears and lies aside, I don't really* know
who I am. I've barely been keeping my head above water
for years. Between the diapers and the deadlines and the laun-
dry and feeding people and trying to wash my hair at least once
a week, I feel like a robot. A shell of myself. Where do I even
begin? I get it, sister, and it's time to pump the brakes.

To begin, take a deep breath. In the beginning, God
breathed life into man. Deep breathing tells our bodies that it's
okay to pause and that it's time to slow everything down for a
moment.

One more breath.

Good.

Each of us has been gifted with a unique set of talents and abilities. Yes, you too. And throughout our journey to right-here-right-now, we've gathered wisdom from experiences, strength from painful tears, and confidence (at least in a few things) from our own individual challenges. How often do we love and prioritize ourselves enough to give ourselves the gift of a few minutes to reconnect with our beautiful, quirky, fantastic souls?

Maybe you're feeling a little squirmy at this idea. Big and heavy things are going on in the world right now that may make this exercise seem frivolous. Here is one thing I know for sure:

> **Have you ever wondered what your soul might look like?**

Who you are—every big, small, weird, awesome thing about you and where you've been—it *matters*. Enormously. God knew the world needed a big, diverse kingdom of different individuals. And imagine what we might become (how He'd be glorified) if we all grew wildly, with all our crazy colors and differently shaped leaves! What beauty!

Also, maybe it's been a few years since you've done an exercise like this. Well here is one more thing I know for sure:

You've changed.

And that's good! But now it's time to get to know you. The right-now you. The you that has been through hard stuff and dares to hope for a better day. The beautiful, glorious, color-ful you underneath all those layers laid on thick by time and experience.

THE COLOR OF YOUR SOUL

Have you ever wondered what your soul might look like? Stay with me here. I'm a visual person. Marcus Aurelius has been translated as writing, "The soul becomes dyed with the colors of its thoughts."[4] So when I imagine the very essence of who I am, who God made me to be, all the quirkiness and goodness within me brought to life in color, I see beautiful coral pinks, the deepest of Caribbean turquoise blues, a shimmer of chartreuse green running smoothly into a bright golden yellow. There's glitter. Barely though, clinging tightly to colors just enough to add a glimmer of a sparkle and light reflected by the ever-moving hues intermingling with each other.

Your soul never stays the same. It's constantly regenerating and evolving, a colorful mix of joy, elation, gentleness, love, and compassion. It also contains the tenderness of our worries, the softness of our hopes, and even a few beautiful scars from falls we've taken. Your soul holds a love so deep in hue that it can't be expressed in words, a hope so bright that it cannot be captured in a sentence, and curiosities so rare and bubbly that you might miss them if you look away.

How beautiful! And to think, God painted that mystery and wonder and wildness within each of us.

"It takes courage to

grow up and become

who really are."

—*E. E. Cummings*

Through a process of self-discovery, we will reconnect with the you-est you, the wild and ever-evolving heart of your heart, the very unwavering essence of who you are and always will be. Then we'll practice discerning and realigning with God's will, His plan, for our lives—who He is and always will be. His plan may not be entirely clear, perhaps not in the long-term sense (and that's okay), but we'll work to uncover it for at least that next choice you make. You don't have to see the entire journey at once to enjoy the beautiful possibilities in front of you.

This is the place where our innermost dreams intersect with God's great design and the pieces of our path start to fall into place. We'll also discuss what it means to get comfortable with confidence: humbly embracing our imperfections, intentionally working to refine our character, and boldly designing our daily lives to reflect the sure and solid goodness of Christ.

PURELY YOU

I love organizing and lifestyle stuff and making a house a home and creating chore charts, meal plans, and bucket lists. I'm a neat freak. I'm a hopelessly uninterested cook. I love nachos and won't touch a boiled egg with a ten-foot pole. I've seen snow twice. Maybe three times. I've had my heart shattered, my faith questioned, and the rug pulled out from under me. I've birthed three miracle babies, earned my stretch marks, and had surgery when I was a kid to repair a weak muscle in my left eye that was causing it to turn slightly. Yep, I got called cross-eyed.

A lot. It hurt. I worry about my weight, am a true introvert, and sometimes lose my temper. I love historical fiction, Harry Potter, and have a giant collection of ginger jars. I'm shy in large social situations and believe in equality for all. I'm not sure I fit into either political party, and I make my bed every single morning, no matter what.

I tell you all of these very random tidbits about myself to show you that I'm just as complicated and quirky as you are. We all are. I believe God designed us as incredibly complex creatures for a reason. We each bring something unique and different to the world. The secret to being successful (and, if you ask me, happy) is figuring out who you are and embracing it.

A few years ago, I took an online test to discover my enneagram type (find my favorite test at yourenneagramcoach. com). The test was a series of questions that determine where your personality most likely fit one of nine types. I was skeptical at first but thought it might be fun to answer a few questions about my thought processes and motivations, so I went for it.

The result? Spot on.

Enneagram Type 2: The Supportive Advisor. At your best, you are loving, compassionate, and nurturing. At your worst, you are indirect, possessive, and needy.

It was crazy to see myself like that. It was all so true! I continued to read about the Type 2s strengths and weaknesses—who they are when they're at their healthiest and who they are when they're unhealthy. It felt like pulling back the curtain and peeking into my heart from an outsider's perspective. In particular, I was floored by what my results said about my greatest fear, and I think it's a truth that can be applicable to many of us at some point in our lives, regardless of our enneagram number: a core fear of "being rejected and unwanted, being thought worthless, needy, inconsequential, dispensable, or unworthy of love."[5]

Purely yourself.

Nailed it.

Stepping boldly into the strength and spirit you have, by birthright, means knowing that you—yes, you—are *beloved just as you are*.

It means embracing random, awesome, captivating you as you are, unapologetically.

It means cherishing what makes you tick, saying no to what drains you, and nurturing what makes you feel alive.

My understanding of my faith is that you can't do a single thing to earn or un-earn God's love. He loves us wholeheartedly and without condition. He loves us for our imperfections and because of our imperfections, and it's through Him that we have true opportunities to grow.

The anxiety. The addiction. The regrets. The should-haves. The eating disorder. The time you drank too much. The time you ate an entire box of Girl Scout cookies alone when no one was watching. The sins of your past. God sees. God knows. And God still loves you fully and entirely and will walk beside you as you emerge from who you are and step into who you were made to be.

Let's get to know *that* girl. The good, the bad, the stuff that's hard to talk about. Every part of you matters and every part of you makes up who you are right now. First, we'll identify who you are—not to put you in a box or place a label on your forehead—but to spend some time with yourself, acknowledging every inch of you, honoring every part of what makes you *you* and areas in which you can grow. This is our starting line.

First things first, God delights in you.

You know that feeling when you're falling in love and it feels *just so good* for the one you love to love you back? To delight in everything about you? That is how Jesus feels about us, His Bride.

I love this verse because it reminds me how tenderly God cares for us—despite, regardless of, even though, nonetheless. He takes delight in the big and small parts of us and cherishes us in our troubles.

A BOOK ABOUT YOU

When I was a little girl, I was given a book titled *My Book About Me*. I still have it. I taped my school photo to the front and answered all the questions inside in my best handwriting. The questions ranged from topics like favorite colors, to someday dreams, to best friends, to special memories. It was fun to complete and gave me an unexpected sense of confidence. *Look at this girl! She's smart, quirky, ambitious, and interesting.*

I remember enjoying the process, being given permission

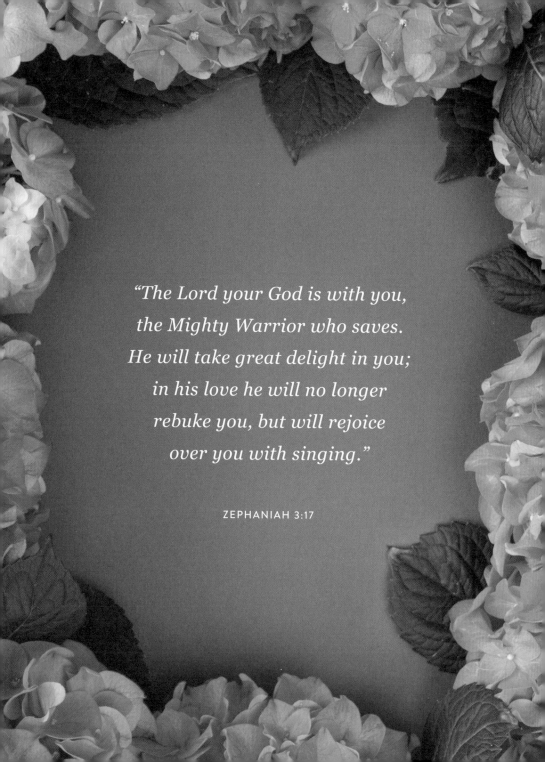

"The Lord your God is with you,
the Mighty Warrior who saves.
He will take great delight in you;
in his love he will no longer
rebuke you, but will rejoice
over you with singing."

ZEPHANIAH 3:17

to spend a little time focusing on a wild and crazy character: me! Flipping through the pages now gives me a sweet snap-shot of little bitty Emily . . . how much joy I found in my mom's tacos (the shells from the yellow box only) and the dream that I would, of course, be a teacher one day.

I wonder, looking back on that book thirty years later, what that kind of self-reflection might do for the girl I am now? For the girl you are? Could this exercise perhaps embolden you a bit to be a little more unapologetically you? Could it help you identify ways you'd like to grow, memories and experiences that made you who you are, joys you'd like to tap back into, and traits that define who you are as a reflection of God?

Spend some time with the following set of questions, and allow yourself to wander to the deepest tucked-away spaces in your heart and soul. The questions range from elemental to elaborate, from tactical to whimsical, each one as important as the next. Some are meant to be lighthearted and fun—to tap into your awesome individual quirks. Some are meant to be thought provoking—to encourage you to dig deep. Answer truthfully (no one but you has to see this), and be as specific as possible. If you feel as if you don't want to write the words that come to mind, that's a clue that you probably *should* put them on paper. Whatever the answer is, silly or sad, basic or beautiful, proud or painful, give it a name. Ownership will begin in your mind, will stir your soul, and will be released into the world through your pen.

Favorites

You are a multifaceted, complex woman. This is a chance to get to know yourself again. Have fun with this. Who are you, right now, right where you are? What's your favorite:

Color	Movie
Food	Book
Sport	Hobby
Weather	Holiday
Season	Memory
Friend	Feature
Quote	Vacation spot
Gift	Hero
Heirloom	Outfit
Animal	Meal
Quiet place	Team
Song	Dessert

My Story

Your journey to where you are right now is important.
You have traveled a beautiful and challenging road.
Write your most transformational stories here.
Embracing where we've been is the best way to dream
about and plan for where we want to go.

_____

_____

_____

_____

_____

_____

_____

_____

_____

_____

_____

_____

We are shaped by the people in our lives, both positively and negatively.
Describe your people below.

Who is your best friend? How did you meet? What does this person mean to you? Why is she your best friend?

_____

_____

_____

Who has been the most positive influence in your life? What did this person teach you?

_____

_____

_____

Who has been the most negative influence in your life? In what ways?

_____

_____

_____

If you could meet anyone, who would it be? What questions would you ask them?

_____

_____

_____

Home is where we rest, rejuvenate, and reconnect. It's often where we are most comfortable, our own space in the world. Describe your home in the spaces below.

I feel most comfortable when . . .

_____

_____

_____

Home is where . . .

_____

_____

_____

This is what I love about my home:

_____

_____

_____

The world is big and you are an important part of it.
Consider your place among all God's people.

This is what I bring to the world:

_____

_____

_____

If I could change one thing in the world, it would be . . .

_____

_____

_____

The most valuable thing in the world is . . . (there are no wrong
answers here)

_____

_____

_____

*If I could change one thing about **my** world, it would be . . .*

_____

_____

_____

No two journeys look the same. We each have unique memories of joy, pain, triumph, and tragedy. These experiences shape who we want to become and who we do not want to become.

The happiest moment of my life so far was when . . .

_____

_____

_____

My proudest accomplishment is . . .

_____

_____

_____

I have experienced heartbreak through . . .

_____

_____

_____

My tears generated strength in me by . . .

_____

_____

_____

Naming fear does not make it stronger. By naming your fears and outlining your worst-case scenarios, you diminish the power they have over you.

I am afraid . . .

_____

_____

_____

_____

_____

_____

_____

The worst possible thing that could ever happen is . . .

_____

_____

_____

_____

_____

_____

_____

This part should bring a giant smile to your face. Write down all the things that bring you joy—all the unique, special, detailed, tiny things you love. Chunky baby laughs. Good coffee in your favorite mug on the back porch. Your mama's lasagna recipe. The smell of the beach. Ridiculous knock-knock jokes. Ready, set, go. Have fun.

I love . . .

_____

_____

_____

_____

_____

_____

_____

_____

_____

_____

_____

_____

_____

_____

_____

_____

_____

Growth happens both quickly and slowly as the days of our lives pass by. How have you grown and changed in recent years? What experiences fueled those transformations?

I have grown . . .

_____

_____

_____

_____

_____

_____

_____

_____

_____

_____

_____

_____

_____

_____

_____

_____

_____

_____

Gratitude changes everything. Take a few minutes to write down what you are truly grateful for: blessings, lessons learned, trials, opportunities, freedoms, people, experiences, memories. Whatever your heart is thankful for, write it down here.

I am grateful for . . .

This is what matters most

I WANT TO SHOUT OUT, DO WHAT
YOU PLEASE, FOLLOW YOUR STAR,
BE ORIGINAL IF YOU WANT TO BE
AND DON'T IF YOU DON'T WANT
TO BE. JUST BE NATURAL AND GAY
AND LIGHTHEARTED AND PRETTY
AND SIMPLE AND OVERFLOWING
AND GENERAL AND BAROQUE . . .
AND LEARN AND LEARN AND
LEARN. OPEN YOUR MINDS TO
EVERY FORM OF BEAUTY.

—*Constance Spry*

I hope you enjoyed getting to know yourself a bit better. I want you to note that we didn't discuss goals in these questions. At this point in the BUILD process, we're simply looking inward, not forward. We're taking a snapshot of who we are—right now. God delights in you. You may have had a few *aha* moments journaling through the previous pages, but God already knew what

> God delights in both who you are and who you are becoming.

you'd write. Let's applaud the time we've taken to reflect and to consider who we are and *whose* we are. You are unique. No experience was wasted in the making of who you are. And God delights in both who you are and who you are becoming.

• • •

My son and I were recently in a local grocery store. An older man, probably in his mid-eighties, was behind us in line. He smiled at Brady and we got to talking. He told us about a time when he was little, about Brady's age, growing up in the Great Smoky Mountains of Tennessee, and he caught a toad. He was enamored with this little toad—its bumps and colors and big eyes. He loved it and became very interested in animals from that point on. Decades later, that little toad-catching boy from Tennessee founded what is now the beautiful fifty-acre Gulf Breeze Zoo in Gulf Breeze, Florida. All because he caught a toad. You just never know what will be sparked by a little curiosity in your heart.

Jessa Bray, Simplified's art director, who painted the cover (and many pages!) of this book didn't go to school to learn to paint. In fact, she never really dreamed of becoming an artist. Instead, her passion found her deep in the deserts of Odessa, Texas, lonely and hurting. Jessa's story is so lovely to me, not because it played out perfectly but because something beautiful blossomed in the middle of the driest season. I'm honored to have Jessa share her story with you here, in her own words.

·   ·   ·

My husband, Tyler, and I welcomed our son, Leland, in early 2015. The early days of motherhood were not full of bliss. Instead, we were fearful that our marriage was falling apart and that we'd have to split custody over a newborn baby. In late April, we packed everything we owned in the back of our Dodge Ram pickup and made the long drive from Virginia to Texas for Tyler to begin a new job. We were terrified to leave everything we knew but were convinced that a fresh start would help us draw closer together.

I'll never forget pulling up to the dingy orange apartment complex in the desert of Odessa, Texas. I felt so out of place and so alone. Leland was crying in the backseat, another reminder that my body was not producing enough milk for him. I had never felt further from myself than in that moment. I had never felt further from God, my family, my friends, or my husband either. Over the next few months, Tyler drove our only vehicle to work while I stayed home and learned how to be a mom. Every day, I pushed a stroller in circles in our parking lot (to avoid the gang activity outside our complex), sat with Leland next to our half-empty apartment pool, and nursed and changed him. When Leland napped, I'd doodle, drawing letters and writing words in pretty ways. It was all I had to pass the time.

On the weekends, I'd walk local stores and see so many beautiful art pieces and pillows. I couldn't afford them, but I longed to have beautiful things in our apartment, to make the orange place in the desert of Texas a home. I wondered if I could make something beautiful for our home with what I had. I began looking for videos about how to make things, how to draw in a beautiful way, and eventually, how to paint.

We lived in a one-bedroom apartment, so late at night I'd go into our bathroom while Leland slept in a Pack 'n Play outside the door, pull out my pen, and practice, practice, practice. I wrote scripture over and over. I was raised in the church and knew more scripture than quotes, so that's where I started. Every time I practiced, I felt the distance between God and me shrink . . . bit by bit. I began sharing my creations on

Instagram, and friends encouraged me to open an Etsy shop.

One night, as Tyler and I lay in bed discussing the day, my phone made a weird *cha-ching* sound. Someone had purchased one of my amateur prints. One sale turned into many. Many turned into enough to pay our power bill. Then our rent. And eventually, those *cha-ching* sounds turned into a sustainable amount to live on. Hours of lettering sparked a fire to seek the Lord with my whole heart, and before I knew it—years and hurdles and so much practice later—I had a thriving business and a restored marriage. I never set out to become an artist. I have no background or formal training in art. Never in my wildest dreams would I have imagined seeing the words *art director* next to my name.

I've never felt more like the woman I was made to be than now. Painting and lettering infuse my world with color and life and meaning. What a precious gift from a very gracious God.

Whether you've fully answered the questions on the previous pages or plan to circle back when you have some quiet time, I hope the time of reflection is both fruitful and renewing. Let us remember that our imperfections are part of the complex fabric of our souls and that each one is calling us to draw nearer to the perfection found only in Christ.

benediction

May you allow God to lead you toward

your calling each and every day,

embracing who you are, where you've

been, and where you're headed.

Dare to trust that the path before you

may be hard, but it will be worth it.

reflection

What unique delight did you discover

or rediscover through this process?

Beginning with the words "I am,"

make a brief, bold statement about yourself,

even if it's a little hard to believe right now.

3

GET COMFORTABLE
WITH CONFIDENCE

She was one of the rare ones. So effortlessly
herself and the world loved her for it.

ATTICUS

I have a little boy named Tyler. Tyler Joseph. We didn't intend to give him the initials T. J. No, in fact, he was named first after a cute name we found while searching the internet (Tyler) and second after his great-grandfather (Gene Joseph— hardworking, loving father to my mom). Still, we hope one day he'll go by T. J.

T. J. Ley just has such a ring to it.

Tyler is quirky and awesome—the first of my twins to be born. Caroline followed three minutes later, kicking and loudly entering the world with her signature high-pitched wail. From his first moments, Tyler has been my mellow kid. A teddy bear. He is sweet and kind, as gentle as they come. We say he's made out of marshmallows and honey. He's a string bean of a kid— wiry and good as gold.

On any given day, you'll find Tyler wearing Spider-Man pants, his favorite popcorn shirt (a kernel of popcorn diving into a bucket of butter), and a Pokémon hat on sideways. It's his signature look, and I love it. When you ask Tyler a question, he affirmatively responds with, "Yip." It's become a favorite phrase for the Ley family. Every night, when I tuck him in, he says, "Good night, precious mama." And he won't allow me to shut the door until I respond, "Good night, precious baby."

Sometimes, in the middle of a crazy game of who-knows-what with his older brother and twin sister, Tyler will pause, look at me with his great big blue eyes, and simply, matter-of-factly state, "I need some alone time now, Mom." Then, much to the bewilderment of his nonstop brother and sister, off he'll go to a quiet place with his favorite plastic box of mismatched Legos. Happily solo, Tyler will build his creations—sometimes a car shaped into a spider with legs that bend and move, sometimes a city with tiny little flowerpots adorning every window ledge. He leaves no detail unattended, carefully placing each tiny Lego just as it should be. It's his happy place when he needs it, and when he's filled back up with whatever he finds during his alone time, he rejoins the party.

> To be effortlessly you is to refuse to boast *and* *also* to refuse to shrink.

Though he's just five, Tyler is a confident kid—blissfully unaware of the rest of the world and markedly self-aware for a little guy. I see assuredness in him—an unapologetic state of being simply who he is. Maybe it's because he's a kid, unaffected by the grown-up world. Or maybe it's one of those things God gifted him with—the confidence to be so effortlessly himself. You can learn a lot from kids, you know.

May we all have the confidence to be so effortlessly ourselves. To drop the baggage of who we used to be, who we thought we'd be, who our families wanted us to be, who the world says we should be . . . to simply be us. Imperfect and growing. Messy and kind. Smart and savvy. To confidently seek out what we need. The truth is that to be effortlessly you is to refuse to boast *and also* to refuse to shrink.

DONE PLAYING SMALL

Maybe it's because I'm pushing forty. Or maybe it's the buckets of experience I've had as a scrappy entrepreneur, but I'm done playing small, shrinking or dimming to make others comfortable. You too? This is fire, y'all, and I feel it so strongly. I'm ready to say hard things, to be proud of my achievements, and to press into the uncomfortable for the sake of hope and what could be.

You weren't made to play small. You weren't made with a light that requires dimming for the comfort of others. No way, no how. When you achieve a goal, celebrate. When you fail, apologize. And when you are afraid, lean into it, name it, hold it, and then set it aside. When you feel those slivers of confidence bubbling up, grab hold of them. The world needs who you are.

What it looks like to be *effortlessly me* . . .

_____

_____

_____

_____

_____

_____

_____

_____

Confidence isn't the aura of someone who has come out on top every single time. Confidence comes when we learn a truth about life, about the nature of people, about the character of God, and about strength we didn't know we had.

If I sat in front of each of you and asked how you discovered whatever sliver or slice of confidence you have, when you really began to trust that God's got this and trust your gut, you'd probably each tell me about a hard thing. A season of struggle. A time when you were torn down . . . to be built back up. Or maybe you'd tell me you don't yet know. Confidence has escaped you and you're searching desperately to know *one thing with certainty.*

I once heard writer and speaker Priscilla Shirer say, "We are all in one of three places. We're either right smack in the middle of something, coming out of something, or on our way into something. But this is where we get to know the glory of God."[6] The hard times are when we have to lean on Him, trusting that He will build us back up, that He will resurrect us from the rubble, that He will breathe life back into us when all seems lost . . . this is where our confidence is unearthed. And you better believe I will wear my hard-won confidence proudly. Through difficult stuff and the challenging stuff, the triumphs and the tragedies, coming undone and being put back together, I have fought for and won my confidence. And so have you.

I have made costly business mistakes and faced the challenge of earning that money back so I could try again. (Hard-won confidence now reminds me: you can face hard things and come out the other side.) I have set goals and worked my tail off to achieve them, even if the journey took a really long time. (Hard-won confidence now reminds me: if you dare to do the work, the end result can be yours). I use this hard-won confidence to strengthen my resolve as I step into the next season of life. Won't you come alongside me?

Oprah Winfrey was once asked by renowned film critic Gene Siskel to share what she knew for sure. She was caught off guard and fumbled for her words. Finally, she said, "I'm not sure. But I'm going to spend some time figuring that out."[7] Whether you're in Oprah's shoes or standing firm in your truths, here are a few things *I* know for sure that I'd like to share with you.

1. You were not made to play small.
2. Your life, no matter what it looks like, has profound significance.
3. God won't let you down. You can trust Him. You can also trust your gut. He's in there too. I fully believe that when we are filling our hearts with truth, our gut feelings can often represent the urgings of the Holy Spirit.

Go be effortlessly you. Wear those big feather earrings. Go spend some alone time with your Legos. Get lost in those books you love. If you like that Pokémon hat sideways, girl you wear it proudly. Does it make you uncomfortable for someone to tell you that you can go and do the thing? That you can own the thing? That you can achieve all that stuff on your heart? Turn that noise down. Get comfortable with your confidence. In the coming chapters, we're going to dig into the delicate balance between hustle and rest and what it means to work smart. First things first, you be you. The world needs you.

> The only person you are destined to become, is the person you decide to be.
>
> RALPH WALDO EMERSON

benediction

May we embrace all sides of ourselves—deep and surface, forward and behind us, within and around us. May we find beauty in our imperfections and grace in our shortcomings. May we confidently, boldly proclaim that we have what we need to take that next step forward. May we go bravely into tomorrow, assured that we can be effortlessly ourselves and be more than enough in the light of God.

reflection

What does being effortlessly you look like?

Pretend a friend asked you to write a one-paragraph biography for her, to be read before she is introduced on a stage somewhere, boasting her achievements and the obstacles she has overcome. Except that friend is actually you. Get comfortable with confidence here. It's okay to own it.

Leaving excuses at the door, honoring where you've been, who are you becoming?

BUILD

Utilize what you have.

Part Two

Theodore Roosevelt once said, "Do what you can, with what you've got, where you are."[8] Let's add a little fire to that: "I will take that next step, using everything I already have, beginning where I am right now, right in the thick of things." That statement takes boldness. No matter where you've been, consider where you are *right now*. What do you already have that you can utilize to strengthen your resolve, color your spirit, and underline your boldness? Consider your gifts, your virtues, and your experiences. Allow both the good and bad to come together as intertwined muscle to strengthen the woman you are becoming—the woman who will build a life she loves.

You are in control. In the next three chapters, we'll dig in to how we navigate the hard stuff of life to come out stronger on the other side.

"DO WHAT YOU CAN,

WITH WHAT YOU'VE GOT,

WHERE YOU ARE."

—*Theodore Roosevelt*

4

DIG UP YOUR GRIT

Enthusiasm is common. Endurance is rare.

ANGELA LEE DUCKWORTH

While teaching seventh-grade math, Angela Duckworth realized that some of her brightest, highest-IQ students were performing poorly on tests. Conversely, some of her lowest-IQ students were making fantastic grades. Since the IQ test is the standard measurement tool used to predict eventual academic success, she was puzzled. Despite their current grades, she was convinced that each student in her class could learn decimals, fractions, and ratios, so she left the classroom to earn a graduate degree in psychology. She has since devoted her academic career, as a professor at the University of Pennsylvania, to studying why some people are successful and others are not and to ask the question: If IQ, or "genius," doesn't predict eventual success, what does?

Duckworth and her researchers studied cadets at West Point (Who would be most likely to graduate? Who would drop out?), children at the National Spelling Bee (Who would make it to the finals? Who would not?), and even students in Chicago Public Schools (Who would perform despite their socioeconomic status, and who would not?). Duckworth's team discovered, when combining years of diverse data, that one factor above all else (race, gender, finances, family makeup, IQ, and so on) was the key predictor of success in a person: *grit*, a unique combination of passion and long-term perseverance.[9]

The level of grittiness you have determines how successful you will be at achieving your goals.

If that's the case, how do I get more grit?

Duckworth says she is often asked this question. She explains that data has shown a direct correlation between a person's level of grit and whether or not they operate with a growth mindset. A growth mindset simply means that we're not afraid to get back up when we fall down, and we acknowledge that "as much as talent counts, effort counts twice."[10] We know that failure isn't final. Failure is simply a stepping stone, a challenge we encounter on our way to an end goal. Grit is grown over time. Grit is strengthened by challenges, not chipped away by them.

> Failure isn't final. Failure is simply a stepping stone, a challenge we encounter on our way to an end goal.

Duckworth explains that grit grows when we live by the "Hard Thing Rule." The Hard Thing Rule is that we must do one hard thing every single day.[11] Reading this made me smile and think of my friend Christi's story from chapter 1 and her family's motto: "We do hard things."

When we routinely tackle hard things, grit is cultivated within us. If Duckworth's research is right (and I believe it is), we can stop asking ourselves if we have enough money, enough intelligence, enough connections, or the right plans to be successful in achieving our goals. Instead, we can start putting our grit to good use and doing that next hard thing.

Instead of, "Do I have enough *education*?" ask yourself, "Am I willing to put forth enough *effort*?"

Instead of, "Am I *smart* enough?" ask yourself, "Am I *savvy* enough to learn?"

Instead of, "Do I have enough *talent*?" ask yourself, "Am I *tenacious* enough to fight for it?"

Instead of, "Will this be *easy* enough?" ask yourself, "Am I *scrappy* enough to problem-solve my way through the hard stuff that will come along the way?"

Instead of, "Will this be *hard work*?" tell yourself, "*This will be hard work* and *I am worth it*."

Perhaps you've been waiting to build a life you love because you're waiting for the time to be right, for the stars to align, or for that winning lottery ticket to land in your lap. I'd challenge you to look at your own level of grit. Do you have it in you? Angela Duckworth says you do. I think you do too. Grow it. Cultivate it. Do today's hard thing.

Mark Twain has been quoted as saying, "If it's your job to eat a frog, do it first thing in the morning." I cannot stop laughing at this! But isn't it so true? If you have to do a hard thing, tackle it first thing, head on. Just get it done. The grit that is

What hard things have you been avoiding? They're different for all of us! What's hard for me might be a breeze for you. Let's make a list so we can eat that frog.

_____

_____

_____

_____

_____

_____

_____

developed by going scared and facing something challenging head-on is so valuable.

Anyone you know, anyone you see, who has become someone you admire, something that person is proud of, has put in work. They've eaten some frogs for breakfast! They've developed their grit. Perhaps all you see from the outside is who they are *now*, not all the work that went into the person they have become. That person was probably afraid at some point (I know I was). That person was probably exhausted at some point (definitely). And that person is probably dang sure glad she stuck it out (hand raised high in the air!).

GUMPTION, GRIT, AND GRACE

In interviewing women as I prepared to write this book and in digging through my own experiences with facing my fears and growing boldly despite the obstacles, I came across three virtues all successful women seem to have in common: they put to work their gumption, grit, and grace. Successful women have the gumption to believe that they are deserving of a life they love, the grit to dig in and make things happen in the face of whatever life has thrown at them, and the grace to roll with the punches and accept their own imperfections.

What follows the process of self-discovery (understanding who you are, aligning yourself with God's calling in your life, and getting comfortable with the confidence you've fought for) is *action*. Building a life you love requires that you *do something*. It doesn't mean we must have a perfect plan in place; it simply means we have to put one foot in front of the other, prayerfully, thoughtfully, and with bravery. Even if we're unsure, even if we're scared, we build. We act in faith. We work and act from a place of love.

> Building a life you love requires *that you do something.*

1. GUMPTION

When Bryan and I were first married, we decided we wanted to grow our family pretty quickly. A period of infertility followed, but thanks to the advice of our specialists, Brady Ley was born. A few years later, we decided we wanted to add a second child to our family. We were unsuccessful for three years—even through multiple, seemingly endless rounds of treatments. (Side note: "unexplained infertility" is a real pain of a vague diagnosis.) Eventually our doctor told us that our only option was IVF: in vitro fertilization. It was expensive and complicated. Still, the doctor thought our chances were good. We set aside some months from our desire to have another baby to save up for the procedure and to pray about it. We decided we would give it one try.

And so I did the obvious next thing: nothing.

I could not bring myself to make the call to schedule that first in vitro appointment. Making the call should have been so simple, right? It was a matter of dialing a phone number and scheduling an appointment. But to me it was so much more. It was embarking on a path with an unknown destination— something I am *not* comfortable with. Instead of making the call, I spent months grieving that this was our journey (which was okay, by the way!) and also dwelling on what we *didn't have*—another baby, a sibling for Brady.

I couldn't seem to take that next step. Until one day, my good friend handed me my phone and said, "You've made the decision. Now make the call." I dug up the tiny bit of gumption I had in me and did the next right thing. I dialed the number for our specialist's office, heart racing, palms sweating, thoughts spinning. There was a scrappiness in that decision. A sense of going scared.

2. GRIT

A whole crazy process followed that first appointment. It took a lot of grit (not to mention an enormous financial investment). Every day I took medication that caused massive hormone swings, gave myself painful shots, and endured constant procedures and exams all with the knowledge that it might not actually work. But isn't that what grit actually is? Going scared? Going hopeful anyway? And so, I abided by my doctor's detailed instructions and waited anxiously (nerves on fire) for daily updates from the clinic. We also discussed the worst-case scenario: the very real possibility that the treatment might not work. But we pushed forward. Because we couldn't be successful in it if we didn't at least try.

I'll never forget hearing "there are two heartbeats" while lying on the exam table in the specialist's office. (God apparently had big plans for our family: not just one baby conceived nontraditionally but two!) I thought Bryan might faint. And I was elated. Carrying twins taught me a lot about grit and how much mental determination is also connected to physical strength. My body went through a lot over the next few months—from ovarian hyperstimulation to ovarian torsion and more. I spent a total of twenty-two days in the hospital and more than six weeks on bedrest. But I fought for those babies with all the grit I had.

3. GRACE

Tyler and Caroline joined our family a little more than nine months after that first phone call. Looking back to the day

I finally dug up the gumption to pick up my phone is somewhat mind-blowing. Tyler and Caroline wouldn't be here had I not made that terrifying call. But let's talk about that worst-case scenario. The tricky parts of our journeys are where grace comes in. Would I have grown regardless of how the scenario played out, regardless of whether I had conceived? I believe I would have. I did a hard thing. There would have been a lot of grief involved, but I know that God would have met me in those moments to continue to shape who I was becoming regardless of the outcome.

I want to reach out a hand here if you are feeling especially stuck. Perhaps the idea of digging up gumption, grit, and grace feels like it requires a tenacity you simply don't have. It's in these very uninspired and uncertain moments when we have to sit down, turn down the noise, and put a name to what's holding us back. Being stuck like this is like refusing to close your eyes at night because you're sure there's something scary in the dark. Turn the light on. Look around. Name your fears (What does the monster look like? Is it even there?). Giving the glue that's keeping you stuck a *name* will provide the specificity and the detail to come up with a way to overcome it. And remember: overcoming it doesn't always mean winning a battle or crushing a goal. Sometimes overcoming a fear or a stuck feeling means taking one step out of place, removing yourself from where you're stuck.

If we simply have the tenacity to free our forward movement from the shackles of doubt and fear, we will fan the flame

IF YOU CAN'T FLY,

RUN.

IF YOU CAN'T RUN,

WALK.

IF YOU CAN'T WALK,

CRAWL.

BUT BY ALL MEANS,

KEEP MOVING.

—Dr. Martin Luther King Jr.

> Find that flame, fan it wildly, and put to work the spirit inside you.

within us, even if it's the tiniest of glowing embers right now. What a gift to have a few ounces of fire within ourselves, regardless of the rest of our lives. Find that flame, fan it wildly, and put to work the spirit inside you. You never know what might happen.

benediction

May you never doubt that a powerful spirit and a whole lot of
grit lie inside you. And when the doubts creep in, consider this:
Your growth doesn't have to look like massive growth or quick
transformation or sudden success. Your growth can be bold
even when growing slowly and thoughtfully. Either way, grow
in the right direction, and "by all means, keep moving."[12]

reflection

Reflect on a time when you had to rely on sheer
grit to get you through to the other side. Where did
that grit come from? What did it feel like?

What is the next right thing for you? Is it a
phone call? A text message? Maybe it's a nap?
Sometimes it takes grit to put yourself first.
Write it down.

What fears are holding you back? Be specific.

Grit is a direct result of having purpose that is special. Define
your purpose for building the life you want to have here.
How can you commit to grit when things get hard?

5

STAND STRONG ON YOUR STORY

*In all ranks of life, the human heart yearns for the beautiful; and
the beautiful things that God makes are his gift to all alike.*

HARRIET BEECHER STOWE

When we think of beauty, we automatically think of something pleasant to look at. But real beauty is often much more complex than that. Sometimes beauty is a lesson learned. Sometimes it's a dream realized. Sometimes it's a story come full circle—pain that eventually holds spiritual meaning and moments of delight found in the nooks and crannies of otherwise difficult circumstances.

NOTHING IS WASTED

Shortly after he started high school, my younger brother, Brett, brought home a beautiful girl to introduce to me and my parents. She was quiet, strong, and warm as could be. We immediately bonded over our favorite hair products, of course, future sisters-in-law in the making.

> Sometimes pain eventually holds spiritual meaning, and moments of delight are found in the nooks and crannies of otherwise difficult circumstances.

Taylor immediately became part of our family. But it would be years before I learned more about what she'd experienced before she officially became one of us— the challenges and pain that had shaped all sides of her beautiful, scarred, strong spirit. Taylor boldly and graciously allowed me to share her story here in hopes that those of you who may be walking difficult paths beyond your control will be encouraged to recognize your own strengths and to believe in the beauty that is to come. I'm grateful to Taylor for her bravery in sharing these sacred stories, and I hope my tender delivery honors who she's become despite and because of her circumstances.

When Taylor was just five years old, her parents divorced, and her mom moved out of their house. Because her father worked overtime to support their family, often into the evenings, Taylor moved in with her grandparents shortly before starting kindergarten. Her collective family wanted Taylor to experience traditional family life, at her home, regardless of all the moving pieces, so she'd sometimes move back to her father's house, then back into her grandparents' house, when that didn't work as smoothly as hoped.

During this time, Taylor's emotional independence developed—out of necessity. For the things we often rely on our parents for (soothing, comfort, motivation), she primarily relied on herself. And on her grandparents, who remained a constant in her life. Taylor's nana and papa taught her manners, provided traditions, and loved her with all they had. She sought out a relationship with her dad, who was a hard worker devoted to providing for his children the best he could—even if that meant sending her away.

This was all Taylor knew—a disjointed home life, a loving family with her grandparents, a mother she visited twice a month, and a father who did the best he could. Taylor explains that her dad was a loving man but that he had a hard time expressing his emotions. Birthday cards that read simply, "I'm proud of you. Love, Dad," brought tears and meant more to Taylor than the most eloquent sentiments would have.

When Taylor would try living at her dad's again or visiting her mother to find that nuclear family life or child–parent relationship she ached for, she came up empty-handed. These times at home often fell apart, because of problematic people in both homes—some with head lice, drug addictions, or uncontrolled anger. Taylor was once locked in a closet for an extended period of time by a person visiting one of the homes.

Despite her unstable family and home circumstances, Taylor dedicated herself to her schoolwork and became a cheerleader. She might not have realized it at the time, but through positive influences at school and her own determination, Taylor was gathering all the strength she had to build a life she loved—to rise from the ashes of a traumatic childhood (something she vows not to dwell on). She is focused and fiercely dedicated to creating her own loving, stable family life.

And so it was that a beloved high school science teacher told a young boy who was drawing on a desk in the back of the classroom to sit next to the bright, well-mannered girl in the front row. Clearly he was hoping some of Taylor's good influence would rub off on this kid. The two young people clicked, Brett stopped drawing on tables, and together they set off to build a life they loved. They attended college together, got married, and are now the proud parents of a little girl.

Taylor credits Brett and our family, particularly my mom, for encouraging and inspiring her to rise from a situation she could not control—but certainly did not want to repeat. But I believe deep down—and I think she probably knows this too—that Taylor's strength was all part of that little fire within her, the one she was born with, the one that *no one* can put out, the one that was fanned by the winds of adversity and continued to glow with her belief that *it doesn't have to be this way.* Instead of building on a challenge-free childhood, Taylor has grown in resilience born of hardships and self-sufficiency.

To watch Taylor parent her little girl is a marvel. We are blessed to witness a love—beautiful and whole—that has broken the cycle. She plays with Kennedy's hair, reads her stories at night, and cultivates a home that is both safe and loving.

What is your childhood story? How has it shaped you?

_____

_____

_____

_____

_____

_____

_____

_____

You intended to harm me, but God intended it all for good.
GENESIS 50:20

One of the most profound things Taylor has said in the years since she first shared her story with me is that her childhood is not her identity. It is simply the path she has already walked. And she's moving forward with a life built on purpose—caring for her own daughter and kindling a relationship with her mother as well.

Inspired by my mom to become a teacher, Taylor did life-changing work in the classroom for a number of years. Though she lost both her grandparents to illness and her dad to invasive lung cancer, Taylor continued to use her pain to remind kids from all backgrounds that someone loves them. She'd make surprises for her students, sit with them one-on-one to discuss their feelings, and call their homes when they were out sick, just to let them know she was thinking of them.

Taylor's story continues to leave a trail of beauty. I see it in her quiet strength, in her love for my brother, in the way she encourages me, and in the way she adores her little girl. I also see a beautiful bravery in her pursuit of a warm relationship with her mother years later. One trait I adore about Taylor is her propensity to consider the beauty in sadness, the light found in darkness—a less than ideal and sometimes tenuous growing-up situation that blessedly included grandparents who dearly loved and supported her, a father who did his best and whose intentions she could feel, and an older brother to rely upon. Beauty can be found in the cracks and crevices of the hard stuff we experience. God wastes nothing.

Taylor now handles administration for Simplified while caring for her young daughter. She is a gift to our team and is one of the strongest and steadiest women I know. Taylor has found forgiveness, resolve, and fortitude on a path that likely would have crushed others. Her boldness and tenacity is matched with tenderness, warmth, and unconditional love.

When I asked Taylor what she knows for sure about God, she said, "God never let me down, even though a lot of other people did. Nothing in my life has been wasted. I am stronger because of the path I've walked. And my future is what it is because I've trusted Him with it. Trust isn't easy, but He's never let me down."

He will bestow on them a

crown of beauty instead of ashes,

the oil of joy instead of mourning,

and a garment of praise instead

of a spirit of despair.

ISAIAH 61:3

> Your childhood is not your identity. It's the path you've already walked. You can move forward to purposefully build a life you love.

GOD USES IT ALL

As you build the life you want, the way you see your story can either take away energy or fan the flame. You have the power to decide. Like Taylor, you may have experienced hardship and trauma that many of us cannot comprehend. And if you did, I'm so very sorry. The good news is that God can and will use *all* of it. It will take emotional work and determination, but your experiences do not dictate your story!

And remember: standing strong on the story of your childhood—as perfectly imperfect as it may be—doesn't mean approving of or being grateful for everything that's happened to you. Instead, it means rising up and choosing to respond in strength, to be an overcomer—because you are more than what has happened to you. It's also so important to acknowledge that, in some cases, working through trauma with a trained professional—to dig deep into your history, to heal, and to unearth the beauty of who you are now and who you can become—is so beneficial.

Beauty from ashes. Strength from struggle. Resurrection from rubble. God never told us it'd be easy, only that He'd never leave or forsake us (Deuteronomy 31:6). We live in a fallen world, but God promises that we can do *all things* through Christ, who gives us strength (Philippians 4:13).

benediction

May you rise from what's been burned to the ground in your
life, soaking in the healing rain of earned strength and God's
boundless love. May you always remember you were bought
for a price by the One who loves you endlessly regardless
of your past or current circumstances. May your heart be
soothed by a hopeful song of the beauty that is to come.

reflection

What has been burned to the ground in your own life, big or small?

What has risen or bloomed from the ashes of those challenges?

Beauty is often born out of brokenness.
Detail the strength you've found from your own struggles.

6

RAISE YOUR AVERAGE

You are the average of the five people you spend the most time with.

JIM ROHN

This quote has always stuck with me. The people you spend the most time with shape who you are. They impact your priorities, your choices, how you use your hours, even your behavior and mannerisms. According to research by Harvard psychologist Dr. David McClelland, "[the people you habitually associate with] determine as much as 95 percent of your success or failure in life."[13]

Yes, much of your success depends on you and the way you use the gifts God has given you. But external influences affect how—and sometimes *whether*—you achieve your goals. If you are the average of the five people you spend the most time with, how does your average look right now? Do you need to make any changes? Do any relationship problems need to be addressed? Are there friendships it might be time to distance from? People or influences you'd like to add to your circle? Is it time to raise your average?

WHEN THE NUMBERS DON'T ADD UP

Let's explore some simple math. Remember group projects in school? Even if four of you did your best work, if the fifth member slacked, everyone's grade suffered. If you want to raise your average based on the top five people you spend the most time with, those five people should be consistently positive influences. If even one has a negative effect, it brings down the average. And if a few of them are low, you're really in trouble.

Is it time to make some changes? I get it—change can be hard. We worry about hurt feelings, about making new friends, about rocking the boat. But that friend who calls only to complain? Or who incessantly gossips about others? Or is negative and drags you down with her? Or the friend who doesn't listen?

Perhaps it's time to take a hard look at what this relationship brings to your heart and life and to gently and graciously remove it from your top five. Maybe it's time to seek out a new friend who will build you up. Maybe it's a fellow entrepreneur who encourages you to dream big. Maybe it's a fellow mom who understands what you're going through. Or maybe it's a professional influence—a counselor, mentor, or coach who can help you take that next step.

FOR A SEASON

One of the hardest lessons I've learned in my thirty-seven years is that some people are meant to be in our lives for the long

IS IT TIME TO RAISE YOUR AVERAGE?

haul, but some relationships are meant to last only a season. Like a beautiful flower, that friendship is meant to bud, then bloom to be enjoyed and savored. And then, as the petals fade, it is meant to be let go, with gratitude and love. I have said goodbye to friends because of this fact of life. Perhaps it's a matter of proximity. Perhaps it's related to no longer having shared experiences. Some of them still hurt. I choose to look back with affection and gratitude for what they meant to me and what they were.

I had a dear friend during my younger days that I did everything with. Sadly, we grew apart. Eventually we parted ways. And you know what? That's okay. We agreed that we were on different paths and couldn't see eye to eye on things that mattered deeply to both of us. It was time to tie the bow on our friendship, to be grateful for it, and to move on. Not all friendships close this gracefully. Sometimes they simply fade away. And just as life shifts from season to season, that's okay too. The beauty of the truest friendships I've ever had is that I may reconnect with a friend after a few years of a certain season pulling us in opposite directions, but that genuine love for one another is still there. What a gift!

> Show me your friends, and I'll show you your future.
> ANONYMOUS

I was engaged before I met my husband, to the high school sweetheart I dated for ten years. We had many wonderful experiences and really grew up together. We got engaged because it felt like the next step. And then we called it off. We just weren't meant to be married. Our time together was special and important, but God had other plans for both of us. Our relationship served its purpose in both our lives, and though it ended, it sits on the shelf of my cherished memories, a meaningful part of the path I've walked to building the life God has for me.

I have friends who have been dear to me since I could barely speak their names. And some friends have been in my life for just a season. Each is valuable, each special, each one a treasured part of my story, of my average—as I have been for them. You have the agency to control your average, the power to add and remove, with conviction and love.

SOMEONE IN YOUR CORNER

My husband, Bryan, brings up my average. He challenges me, drives me nuts sometimes, and encourages me to step closer to who I want to become. He has also played a massive role in the growth of my company. Let me begin by telling you that Bryan doesn't call me Emily. He calls me Sue. Always has. My middle name is Suzanne, and somehow Emily Suzanne morphed into simply Sue. I love my just-for-him nickname so much that we gave it as a middle name to our daughter, Caroline Sue.

Bryan is lighthearted, whereas I am a worrier. He is a comedian and loves the limelight, whereas I love a deep conversation and prefer to observe. He's also innately gifted when it comes to dollars and numbers and business. Even though he's not on the payroll, Bryan's business savvy has come in handy as we've grown Simplified. He has encouraged me to take risks, has helped me make countless decisions big and small, and has led the financial side with excellence and precision.

At work and at home, Bryan is the boost of confidence when my worries are whirling, the data-sorter when all the moving pieces start to blur together, and the one who reminds me to be brave, but not blind, when making a decision. He's also the one who comforts me when I'm sad but will also look at me crumpled in defeat and say, "Sue, get up." Hearing, "Sue, get up," is like hearing, "Turn that mess down." He means business.

I can't say enough about how important it is to have someone in your corner who will support you softly and also shake your shoulders when you need to be reminded that you're strong and that wallowing or worrying isn't getting you any closer to your goal. This person could be a friend, a mentor, a coworker, or a significant other. If it's true that I'm the average of the five people I spend the most time with, then Bryan has made me a heckuva lot stronger by encouraging me to work my tail off toward who I want to become and what I want to bring to the world.

It's also amazing (and hard!) to have someone in your top five who will tell it like it is when you need to hear it. I know we're talking a lot about strong women in this book, but your top five likely includes a strong man who challenges you and grows you. B, as I call him, is my person. I don't always want to hear his pep talks, like a coach at halftime during the Super Bowl. But he sure does raise my average.

benediction

May you be blessed with a special handful of both lifelong and seasonal friends. May each, a treasure in his or her own right, support you where you are and push you toward where you want to go. May God cross your path with the paths of those whose energy, passion, and entrepreneurial spirits will strengthen yours, and yours theirs. May you be blessed with friends who love you, not in spite of your quirks, but because of them, and who help shine light on your best qualities and God-given gifts. May you be someone who brings the average of others up, and may that goodness point back to the Father who made you in His image.

reflection

Who do you honestly spend the most time with?

How is your average looking currently?

Are you satisfied with it, or would you like to raise your average?

Name a few people (or types of people) you could pull closer to your inner circle or changes you may need to make about how close certain people are to you.

BUILD

Imagine the life you dream of.

Part Three

You've made it to one of my favorite exercises in this book. Now is where we get to say out loud what the good life looks like—for each of us. Maybe the good life for you is running a successful business. Perhaps it's going to your job and then coming home to enjoy your loving family. Or maybe you want to learn to love yourself for the glorious, beautiful woman God made, stretch marks and all. Maybe "the good life" is some combination of many different things. You must be brave enough to say whatever that thing is, to silence the lies holding you back, and name the dream out loud.

Have you ever heard of what Jim Collins calls the "big, hairy, audacious goal"?[14] He likens it to the moon mission of the 1960s. President Kennedy easily could have announced that his goal was to "beef up the space program." Instead, he got specific and bold about something with a fifty-fifty chance of success. "I believe that this nation should commit itself to achieving the goal, before this decade is out, of landing a man on the Moon and returning him safely to Earth."[15] We all know what happened after that.

As you read through the following chapters, think deeply about this: What does a life you truly love look like? And allow yourself to dream!

7

CLAIM YOUR CALLING

*I think that in order to be successful, women have to figure out
what they're passionate about first. No matter what you aspire to,
you've got to love what you do in order to be successful at it.*

MICHELLE OBAMA

I followed a precise road map growing up. Go to college. Get good grades. Graduate from college. Get a good job. Get married. Buy a house. Have children. I checked each box methodically and carefully, then moved on to the next goal. I played it safe, confident in my own hard work to take me from milestone to milestone.

At twenty, I felt proud of my path. It had been relatively smooth and, for the most part, free of significant challenges. My GPA was above average. I'd earned a scholarship. And I had been dating the same boy for years.

What more could I ask for?

By all accounts, this was a happy, safe existence.

My junior year of college, however, my adviser told me I'd need to declare a major and stick to it (I'd been putting it off). I sought the wise and trusted counsel of my parents, and much like I'd done in the past, I modeled my choice after theirs, always aiming to please and make them proud.

As a little girl I'd answered the age-old question "What do you want to be when you grow up?" with dreamy answers like "an artist" or "a ballerina." But as I got older and the structure of life began to set in, those dreams seemed further from my reach and from the realm of reality. My parents and my advisers encouraged me to follow my heart—in ways that were practical.

As a woman, I also considered my future spouse and children when choosing my major. At the ripe age of twenty, I felt as if I was being asked to decide who I would be for the rest of my life. This enormous task sent me into a panic the likes of which I'd never known. I experienced what I can only call an existential crisis. Who was I going to be as a young professional? A new wife? A mother with small children at home (God willing)? Who was I going to be when I was sixty? What schedule suited the woman I would become, and what income would support the life I dreamed of?

So. Many. Questions.

So I did what I knew best: I followed in the footsteps of the woman I admired most, my mom. I borrowed her dream and donned her bravery. I enrolled as an education major the following semester.

My mom wasn't just any teacher. She was the very best kind of teacher. The one who requests to teach the children with the lowest test scores, the least amount of home support, and the greatest need for nurturing. My mom taught using methods she created to help children who learned differently. She stayed late to help older kids finally learn to read. She even quietly brought in clothes for children who had no choice but to wear the same outfit to school day after day. She's an angel of a teacher who graced the classroom for thirty-eight years.

My mom was spiritually gifted for her calling. She was innately good at connecting with students, at helping them face their challenges and embrace their strengths as they grew. She was spirited and bold in her career as a teacher. She fought for resources for her students. She was creative and engaging, inspiring kids of all abilities to be their very best. One year, as she taught a dropout prevention class full of at-risk fourth-graders, she created a mantra she'd have her kids shout after completing a task or achieving a goal or when things just felt hard: "HEY, HEY! I LIKE MYSELF!" It may sound silly, but through those words, the kids learned confidence and boldness in the face of hard stuff. They grew so much because they learned to believe in themselves.

My mom's career as a teacher was kingdom work. It was a calling that impacted the lives she touched in enormously special ways. Her calling was to be in the classroom. She changed thousands of lives through her work, with her hands, through her words, and because of her heart. I wanted to do good, meaningful, passionate work too.

I loved children, so when I declared my major, I thought for sure I would be destined to follow successfully in my mom's

DO YOU EVER FEEL LIKE

YOU'VE FALLEN OUT OF STEP,

LIKE SOMETHING IS OFF

AND YOU'RE NOT SURE

WHAT TO DO NEXT?

OR WHAT TO CHANGE?

OR EVEN IF IT'S OKAY TO CHANGE?

footsteps. But with every assignment, something felt off. I didn't feel excited about the work or connected to it at my core. And I quickly realized that I'd ventured outside of God's calling for my unique life.

Do you ever feel like you've fallen out of step, like something is off, and you're not sure what to do next? Or what to change? Or even if it's okay to change? We all feel this way from time to time, in both big and small ways. I believe this is the Holy Spirit whispering gently to us, inviting us to be still for just a moment and to realign with God's calling for our lives. This nudge asks us to identify what truly lights our hearts on fire, where things feel off, and what those intuitions might be telling us about where God needs us to be.

At the end of that spring semester, I withdrew from my education track. My final two years were upon me, and I had little time to figure my life out, only two months to lean in, to listen, and to discover what I really wanted to do with my life. Who I really wanted to become. What life I would build.

All I knew was that I wanted to be challenged. I wanted to do hard things. I wanted to be creative and to solve problems. I wanted to love my job. I didn't want to hate going to the office every morning, wherever that might be. I wanted a job but, like my mom, wanted the flexibility to be the kind of mother I dreamed of being. But I couldn't find anything like that. What in the world was I going to do?

What I learned surprised me. I took personality tests, met with a career counselor, and sought the advice of trusted mentors. Finally, in a last-ditch attempt to come up with some sort of plan, I went to the local library. I wasn't sure what I was looking for. Maybe a book on great career options or on the most in-demand jobs in the United States that year. Instead, I found Emily Dickinson. I got bored looking at business books that meant nothing to me at the time, so I wandered over to find books I actually wanted to read. I loved literature, poetry, and stories with beautiful meanings behind them.

> So few that
> live have life.
>
> EMILY DICKINSON

It was there, sitting on the library floor with a book of Emily's poetry, that my heart sparked to life. With words, with literature, with books. Those moments stirred the embers of a love that had started when I was a child, grew throughout high school, and had sadly died down in the shadow of that great question: "What noble and responsible thing will you become as an adult?"

It hadn't yet occurred to me that I could and would become a woman of many roles, not just the one that provided a paycheck. I hadn't considered that it was okay, even great, to be defined by so much more than my job. Instead of selecting a major that would define my career (even my life? I didn't know), I decided to let that flickering flame, that love for words and stories, that glowing indication of who God needed me to be in His kingdom, lead the way. All these years later, my talents and my degrees are the *least* of what define me.

I'd like to pause for a moment and acknowledge this

funny metaphor about life. There I was in the library, in the "wrong" section no less, trying to find answers, trying to find my place . . . when really, once I listened to where my heart was calling me among those dusty books, I found my answer. Don't ever ignore those little curiosities in your heart, the tugs that seemingly come from nowhere. That, my friends, is a calling, even if you're not sure what it means. That is the Holy Spirit leading you down a path that may not make sense at first but has the power to unfold into something incredible one day.

That very next day, I declared my major as English. I went brave, but not blind. No, I didn't know what job I would hold one day or how much money I could earn as a lover of stories and wordsmithing. But I knew that if I had been made in the image of God, and God had placed in me a deep love and burning curiosity that led me to those beautiful poems and to my eventual friends Milton, Austen, Chaucer, and Shakespeare, then I was likely on a good path of some sort.

I wasn't sure where this path led (so much for that safe road map!) and could see only about three steps ahead. But I kept walking. It wasn't the "proper," safe path that had been set before me. It wasn't the expected choice for the girl with play-it-safe sensibilities. Rather, it was the path where the grass grew tall, where the road was a little trickier, a bit more winding. It was the choice of a girl who was dipping her toe into bravery, trusting God and her gut to lead her down the path to her own wild, creative, bold calling.

Little did I know that one decision set me on the path to

Create an inspiration board from magazine clippings or photos you find on Pinterest. Don't worry too much about making sure they all align with one another. Just begin pulling. Put them together and begin to identify patterns. This is actually how we develop a new collection at Simplified. You may begin to see many photos of the beach, or of children, or even the color blue.

Perhaps you've pulled images of musicians, of paintings, of beautiful flowers. Notice the common themes and consider what these themes may be saying to you about your life.

_____

_____

_____

_____

_____

_____

_____

_____

_____

_____

_____

_____

_____

founding my company, Simplified, to finding my true calling as a creator, and to eventually writing books. No one could have made that decision for me. I had to decide there was something there, something I wanted. I had to go for it.

How have others' expectations defined your life? Are there expectations you'd like to break free from to embrace a more authentic version of yourself? Have you allowed others to make decisions for you? I want to encourage you to venture off the path you're on if you're feeling stuck, especially if you've never deviated before. It's an exciting place to be.

> It was the choice of a girl who was dipping her toe into bravery, trusting God and her gut to lead her down the path to her own wild, creative, bold calling.

IT'S YOUR DECISION

My very best friend's name is Kristin Winchester. We call her KNW because she is Southern as can be and loves a good monogram. Kristin is fiery. Everyone needs a friend like her. She is a gentle soul, always available to provide a listening ear. And she's feisty and fierce, confident in who she is. Kristin and I met when we worked together about eight years ago. She was so impressive at work, always a step ahead, forever coming up with top-notch ideas, and it was clear she was destined for great success.

In 2017, after many years of infertility, Kristin and her husband, Kyle, found out they were expecting boy-girl twins. Kristin was also editor-in-chief of *Southern Weddings* magazine at the time. After thoughtful consideration, Kristin and Kyle made the very personal decision for her to resign from her job and stay home with their children. It was a complex decision, and yet Kristin knew deep down that this was her calling for this particular season.

I recently asked Kristin about all the feelings that come with making a decision like hers. She considered herself fortunate to even be able to have a choice to begin with. Many women aren't afforded the opportunity to consider leaving their careers for their family. But in her case, there was a decision to be made.

Kristin shared a story that took place in a doctor's office recently. She had been asked to complete a questionnaire with her personal information. One question asked for her occupation. As someone who previously felt defined by her professional titles, this gave her pause. And the words "just a mom" floated slowly through her mind. Yet she thought back to the years she and her husband spent saving and preparing so that this opportunity, this title of "mom" could be hers.

In that moment, she felt even more convinced of the sacred importance of her new title. She might not be negotiating multimillion-dollar projects or leading a team of people, but she was doing what was best for her family. No, she wasn't providing an income. No side hustles, no part-time gigs. Instead, she had both feet planted firmly inside the four walls of her home. And in true Kristin nature, this became her passion. She devoted herself to dinnertimes the same way she devoted herself to planning an event for hundreds. She committed herself to exposing her children to creativity through imaginative play just as fiercely as she'd committed to conjuring up vision boards and creative briefs for days-long photoshoots. She found her calling in this season right where she was. What a beautiful thing.

What I love most about Kristin's story is that she has unapologetically claimed her calling *in this season*. Kristin acknowledges that as her children grow, things may change. But she's relishing every messy, hard minute of toddler life times two right now. Kristin told me this recently:

> I want to be clear that this is such a wildly personal decision. Staying home with my children was what was best for *our* family. We only get one chance at life on this side of heaven. In this season, I have been surprised by God's ever-present reminder that I need to keep my eyes fully on Him because it is so easy for them to wander and for me to start second-guessing my choices. I am constantly reminded that I'm not supposed to make decisions to gain acceptance or accolades from others. I don't need to justify my current path to strangers or

friends. My worth and value are not measured in my ability to answer emails, execute advertising campaigns, change diapers, or make homemade baby food. God loves me beyond my wildest imagination, just as I am, regardless of whether I am presenting to a boardroom full of fancy people or rocking a teething baby or trying to do both at the same time. I only get one opportunity, and I wanted to do it right, to find my lane for this season and plant my feet there.

Amen, sister. Amen. As you read this story, may you fully embrace your calling. Claim it. Go after it. Invest yourself in it wholeheartedly, and don't look back. This is your season, and it's your choice.

"When you're curious

you find lots of

interesting things to do."

—*Walt Disney*

benediction

May you lean away from the question: What is my calling? And lean into the question: What is my curiosity? Be it painting, or cooking, or learning to speak Spanish, my hope is that you will allow your heart to go where it is already inclined. Explore that idea, learn more about that skill, and soak up all sides of it. God's intentions for your calling may be found in the deep green strokes of your brush, the people who gather around your homemade biscuits, or in the experience you have while learning about Spanish culture and heritage. Lean in.

reflection

What is your curiosity? Identify it so you can do more of it. How could the life you love be framed with joys and curiosities? How could you build a life you love that is nuanced with captivating hobbies, interesting books, and people who help you become the best version of yourself? What paths lie ahead of you at this point? Define the one you're already on and the options that lie beside it—is there one that may lead to a life you love?

8

DESIGN YOUR ROAD MAP

Give me six hours to chop down a tree and I will
spend the first four sharpening the axe.

—ABRAHAM LINCOLN

It's wonderful to have a goal. But a goal without a plan will never be achieved. And we can't make a plan until our goal *makes sense.* We also can't take action on that tree until all the shrubs and vines and weeds have been removed so we can actually reach it. Simplify first. Plan second. Execute third.

Now, once you're fired up about where you're headed, you may be tempted to move right into action, but as Abraham Lincoln said, spend some time sharpening your ax first. If he had started swinging a dull axe the minute he was assigned the tree-chopping job, he probably would have spent the entire six hours barely making a dent and getting really sore in the process.

> Simplify first.
> Plan second.
> Execute third.

STATE YOUR GOAL

Write down whatever it is you want to do. Boldly claim it as your own. Run a half marathon? Find a church community? Go back to school? Learn that new skill? In this instance, we'll study the following as an example:

I will run a half marathon.

GIVE YOUR GOAL GRACE, CONTEXT, AND SPECIFICITY

Visualize yourself walking the path from idea to completion. From sitting here right now with that place you want to go in your mind, to tomorrow, to a few weeks from now, all the way to a few months or years down the road when you've successfully achieved what you set out to do. What exactly does your journey look like? How does it feel? How did you do it?

Author and speaker Brené Brown points out in her book *Dare to Lead* the importance of "painting it done" when communicating an idea or goal. This is a technique she uses with her team of researchers at the University of Houston, and it's also powerful when used personally. She and her team would identify a goal of some sort, make a plan, then get to work. But they inevitably encountered hiccups along the way—because the end vision wasn't clear to everyone on the team. They'd have to stop and make tweaks, then stop and fix something.

Finally a staffer said to Brené, "Let's paint done."[16] Meaning, "Tell me what this looks like when it's fully completed and perfected." It was an *aha* moment for Brené and an *aha* moment for me! This is why we struggle with goals sometimes; we haven't visualized the entire end result, just the proverbial trophy we snatch at the finish line.

Once you've got the goal in mind, give your simple goal statement some grace (with realistic parameters), context (with *how* you'll achieve the goal), and specificity (with dates, times, and places). This is your vision. Write this down and tape it to your mirror!

I will complete the 13.1-mile Pensacola Half Marathon on November 6, 2021. I will train every week (daily schedule and distances attached) and focus on good nutrition, so I can run as much as possible and walk when I need to rest.

Yes, ma'am!

Doesn't reading that make you feel like *you too* could complete that half marathon? The statement "I will run a half marathon" makes me want to take a nap and maybe cry! It makes me want to go spend money on fancy running sneakers that will sit in my closet.

But the "painted done" big goal, wrapped in grace-filled context, makes me want to put on my ratty New Balances and hit the pavement to walk as much as I can right now . . . today!

It makes me want to prepare a dinner with hearty veggies and good protein tonight. It makes me want to call my friend who has run a bunch of marathons to ask if I can go out with her one day for a walk/run to glean some tips. Look at me now! Just writing this may have turned Emily Ley into a runner!

ROOT YOUR GOAL IN SOMETHING THAT MATTERS

Now that we have some context, let's root this thing in something with some grit, something lasting and meaningful. Whether your goal is to start a business or learn a new skill or fully embrace your role as a stay-at-home mom, what is it rooted in? What is your *why*? This is a good litmus test. If you can't figure out your why—the connection that bridges the gap between your heart and your head—then it may be time to reassess your goal. This is what will propel you forward when your head tells you you're too tired, it's too hard, and you want to give up. Your heart will kick in and take over. That's a magical moment. Something inside you has been stirred for this dream for a reason. Whatever it is, write it down.

> I will complete the 13.1-mile Pensacola Half Marathon on November 6, 2021. I will train every week (daily schedule and distances attached) and focus on good nutrition, so I can run as much as possible and walk when I need to rest. I'm doing this because I want my body to feel

healthy and because I want to challenge myself—so I have lots of energy and strength to be the best version of myself for me and for my people.

How great is this! That, my friends, is a goal with roots. Let's tackle another one, a little closer to home for me.

> If you can't figure out your why—the connection that bridges the gap between your heart and your head—then it may be time to reassess your goal.

Good: I want to sell my creations online.

Better: I want to sell my creations online so I can build my own full-time job.

Best: I want to sell my creations online so I can build my own full-time job, leave corporate America, and do work I love from home with the flexibility to be the kind of mom I want to be.

Yes!

When I went through this process nearly ten years ago, it may not have been as neat and clean as this. But the steps grew into something big. Let me tell you how it happened.

THE PROCESS IN ACTION

In 2011, shortly after my son, Brady, was born, I found myself completely and totally overwhelmed. I had spit-up all over me, was trying to take care of all the clients I had at the time (I was designing brands for other entrepreneurs), and was also working to make sure my shop orders were taken care of (the Emily Ley Shop, as it was known, sold notepads, wedding invitations, and personalized stationery). I was also trying to keep a mountain of clean laundry in a chair in the living room from toppling over under the weight of itself. In my overwhelm, I decided to put Brady in the car and head to Target in search of something to help me get my life together. Am I the only one who has done this? Enter Target with your magic red cart, ready for whatever life-changing piece of home decor or kitchen towel or pajama set might bring about a fresh start?

On this particular trip I had a goal: I was looking for a planner. My business had two facets to track (branding clients and my online shop), our family had grown to us plus this precious baby, and well, taking care of myself wasn't even a consideration under the weight of everything else.

My meandering led me to the aisle with all the planners. I saw brands I recognized and some I didn't. I flipped through pages and looked over cover options. Some were black and white, some color. Some had flexible covers. Some had hard covers. But *all* of them overwhelmed me. The design was a bit fancy. The layouts weren't right for me. And the features were far more than I needed. The last thing I wanted was for my planner to require me to track the number of glasses of water I didn't drink that day (unless coffee counts).

I didn't have a lot of time to be out with the baby that day, so I headed home—empty-handed and frustrated. I put Brady down for a nap and went into my office (the guest room) to pack that day's orders from my online shop. I gathered a stack of Simplified Notepads to slip into cello sleeves and adorn with my signature gold-foil pineapple sticker. The Simplified Notepads were 5 1/2-by-8 1/2-inch notepads I had designed to track the various lists I kept: to-do lists, meal plans, grocery lists, and more. They were organized in rainbow order (one navy, one teal, one turquoise, etc.), and the design was delightfully minimal and cheerful—my favorite style.

While packing up these notepads, an idea began to simmer. I needed a specific planner, and it didn't exist. Maybe I could take a binder and some paper and use this style I loved for the notepads to create my own planner. Using dividers and notebook paper, just like I'd done when wedding planning, I put together a Simplified Life Binder of sorts. It was for me only, and it *worked* for me. I kept track of every day on a different page of notebook paper and put a simple monthly calendar in the front. After using it for a few months and talking to so many other women like me, I knew I was on to something unique and special.

My binder concept eventually gave way to a laminated-cover

> ### Doesn't God surprise us when we lean in?

spiral-bound planner (emblazoned with a giant monogram no less), then to the first wire-o bound, foil-adorned hard-cover planner of its kind—and the one that eventually won Best New Product (in the desktop category) at the National Stationery Show a few years later. But it didn't happen overnight. I didn't start with the goal to win awards, have a big company, be featured in *Forbes* magazine (That happened! Pinch me!), and eventually be able to write bestselling books. No, had you told me back then that any of this madness would happen, I would have told you that you needed to get your head out of the clouds and come back to reality!

But doesn't God surprise us when we lean in?

My journey started with the desire to make a product for myself that solved a problem, then to offer that product to women like me who were also craving simplicity. Who could have predicted where that would lead? Not me!

It started with a crazy idea: "to create a meaningful, minimal planner that will help women simplify and organize their busy lives because I want to put my best organizational skills to use and because this work makes me happy and will help other women feel capable too."

Designing the road map for the Simplified Planner didn't happen with me claiming that goal, mapping out what the

Start your own road map

I've given examples from my experience. Now you try it!

State your goal.

(Emily's example: make a better planner for myself and others.)

_____

_____

_____

_____

Root it in something that matters.

(Emily's example: provide a little lifeline of organization in the chaos we're all going through, and give people moments of calm and hope. Fill this in here.)

_____

_____

_____

_____

Give it specificity.

(Emily's example: explore formatting, branding, materials, etc.)

_____

_____

_____

_____

product would look like, laying out a ten-year plan, and taking out a business loan.

Oh no.

If it had, it would have looked like me saying something like this:

> Here's my big, crazy idea; here's some context around it; here are a bunch of videos I'm going to watch and things I'm going to google; and here's how I'm going to move toward making this thing happen.

Did I know how to manufacture a planner? Nope, but I had a friend and mentor with a giant printing press, and she agreed to print my first planners for me!

Did I have enough money to print a run of these planners on a large scale? Nope, but I knew I could take on a few extra branding clients and save business revenue for a while until the time was right. Adding debt was a risk I did not want to take. I went slower so I could scale smart.

Did I know how to design a print-ready planner file with pages and a cover? Nope, but I had taught myself Adobe Illustrator, so I could probably use the same Google-sleuthing, YouTube-watching techniques to conquer that as well.

Once I knew what I wanted the end goal to be, I simply took the next right step . . . and then the next . . . and the next after that.

What material resources do I need?

_____

_____

_____

What do I need to learn how to do? How could I do that?

_____

_____

_____

What people do I need to know?

_____

_____

_____

What can I afford to spend on this right now? What is my firm budget, and how will I spend it?

_____

_____

_____

What else . . . ?

_____

_____

_____

As things began to progress, I tacked a few more bits of context around that end goal:

This business will give me, and maybe an eventual team, the flexibility to do life well so that we can do work well. This will never be just a planner company. The day that happens is the day I sell it or walk away. This business will be a resource, a community, and a collection of tools for all women seeking simplicity.

> Once I knew what I wanted the end goal to be, I simply took the next right step . . . and then the next . . . and the next after that.

And guess what! That's exactly what Simplified has become. It thrills me, even all these years later, because it was the fulfillment of one of my deepest dreams: to be able to do a job I love while having the flexibility to be the mom I want to be. What's your deepest dream? What would thrill you to have accomplished many years down the road?

Now, with eight team members beside me and an actual home office space to call my own, I still believe in every single word of our end goal. That's how I know I got something right. Yes, we've made a million and a half mistakes along the way, but by simply deciding what your next right step is, you put one foot in front of the other and make small decisions with intelligence, bravery, and a deep connection to what truly matters most to you. The rest will fall into place if you do that. It may take a long time. It did for me. But keep moving forward.

It's been a long time since that day I stood in Target with a crying baby, completely overwhelmed and not finding what I needed, giving up to go home and cobble together my own planner. A few years ago, I stood in that same Target, with my then seven-year-old, and looked at our Simplified Planner, a collaboration with the well-known planner brand AT-A-GLANCE, on that same Target shelf. From idea. To goal. To hard work. To fruition. To that which laid beyond my wildest dreams. Full circle.

THE NEXT STEP

Once you've solidified your goal with context, grace, specificity, and roots, write down your next step. One tiny step. Then a few more after that. Don't let your mind run away with itself. Instead, force yourself to break down the big goal into tiny, manageable actions, at least a few. Next, identify something that you could rhythmically do every single day to move yourself toward that dream. You may have only fifteen minutes a day to pursue this. You may have eight hours a day. I would bet that if you set aside your distractions (your phone, the television, other commitments that don't matter as much), you have more time than you think. Whatever you've got, give all of it to this goal. Don't be afraid to put in the work.

MY ROAD MAP

1. Here's my big crazy goal.

2. Here's my big crazy goal with context, grace, and specificity. Paint it done. Here's what the good life looks like. Here's what it will look like the day I say, "Look at this, y'all. I made it. Look what God has done."

3. Here's my big crazy goal with context, grace, and specificity, rooted in what matters most to me.

4. Here's my one action step I can take right now to move it forward.

5. Here are a bunch of ideas of people I could call or books I could read or things I could google and learn to make it happen.

6. Here's what I'm going to do every single day to get myself into the habit of constantly moving this forward, one little bit at a time.

7. Finish line:

8. Here's who I'm going to surround myself with to make this happen. (Want to be a runner? Find some runner friends! Want to be an entrepreneur? Find some business-savvy friends! Want to grow your faith? Find some small groups to join!) No one succeeds on an island.

9. Here's how I'm going to take care of myself every step of the way.

The late Kobe Bryant, when asked how he became one of the greatest basketball players in the world, said that it was all the 4:00 A.M. mornings.[17] While other people were sleeping, he was up at 4:00 A.M., practicing. While others were staying up late to watch television, he was going to bed early to prepare for an early wake-up call and practice. To do something extraordinary means you have to break out of the ordinary. I'm not saying you should wake up at 4:00 A.M. But I am saying it's exciting to give yourself permission to make some sacrifices. As financial guru Dave Ramsey says, dare to "live like no one else now, so later you can live and give like no one else."

Maybe what you're after isn't a business or a product or to run a half marathon. Maybe it looks wildly different. Maybe it's going back to school for that degree, mending that relationship, or focusing on your health and finally getting your energy back. Maybe you're after a fresh start, renewed rhythm to life, and more confidence in who you are. Maybe your next step is to make a phone call, schedule an appointment, or simply put on your shoes and take a walk. Whatever it is, go after it with gusto. You don't need anything to get started, just the willingness to conquer that next tiny action step. Consider that the most beautiful flowers grow from the tiniest of seeds. Do that next tiny thing: make the call, send the email, have the discussion. You never know what might grow out of your first step.

Master To-Do List

Looking at the tasks required to achieve a big goal can be completely overwhelming, if not paralyzing. I find it helpful, when creating my road map, to simultaneously create a master to-do list. This can be digital or on paper, whatever suits your fancy. But identify one place where you track all the things you'd like to or need to do as you step toward your goal.

benediction

In considering the benediction for this chapter, I kept coming

back to the words of an Irish proverb and the beautiful

way it parallels the road map toward your goals:

May the road rise to meet you. May the wind be

always at your back. May the sunshine warm upon

your face, and the rain fall soft upon your fields,

and until we meet again, may the Lord

hold you in the palm of his hand.

reflection

Define the good life. What will your "life you love" look like when

you've completed the building of it? Describe your schedule,

your home, your friends, your work, and how you spend your free

time. Embrace goodness in all its minute and ordinary forms.

What excites you about this new goal?

What is your goal rooted in? Why does it matter?

BUILD

Love people well.

Part Four

Kindness counts. When you're not sure how to handle a situation, choose kindness. When you don't know how to respond when someone has wronged or hurt you, choose kindness. When you're not sure if you should help, associate with, or welcome someone to your dinner table, choose everyone. In business, at home, at school, remember that everyone is human. To be human is to feel deeply, to love, to hurt, to want, and to regret. Love the human next to you, in front of you, behind you in the checkout line, across the hall from you at work. Love the human leaving that mean comment on your Instagram feed.

If you're unsure of your next step, proceed in love. In fact, tack that phrase on to the end of everything you do.

- "I've got a ton of work today . . . in love (because my work feeds my family and impacts others positively)."
- "I'm going to have a hard conversation with my child about his behavior . . . in love (because I adore this boy and want to teach him how to make good choices)."

Acting in love, especially when it's hard, is one of the boldest things you can do.

When I imagine the very essence of who I am, who God made me to be, all the quirkiness and goodness within me brought to life in color, I see beautiful coral pinks, the deepest of Caribbean turquoise blues, a shimmer of chartreuse green running smoothly into a bright golden yellow. There's glitter. Barely though, clinging tightly to colors just enough to add a glimmer of a sparkle and light reflected by the ever-moving hues intermingling with each other.

9

LEAD WITH INTEGRITY AND PASSION

I didn't learn to be quiet when I had an opinion. The reason they knew who I was is because I told them.

URSULA BURNS, XEROX CHAIRMAN & CEO

When I was twenty-three, I had a job selling ads in our town's local magazine. I went door to door to different businesses, asking to speak to the person in charge of marketing and advertising. Every now and then I'd make a sale, but for the most part I heard a lot of nos. I didn't mind, because those rare yeses made up for the disappointments tenfold.

While I was working for *Pensacola Magazine*, I was asked to sell ad space for *Northwest Florida's Business Climate Magazine*, which was showcasing a newly proposed development for the downtown district: the Community Maritime Park. You would have thought the Community Maritime Park was a four-letter word. People were either passionately *for* the project (set to include a minor league baseball stadium, shops, restaurants, and more on an otherwise unused plot of land) or vehemently *against* the project (for one political or developmental reason or another). The residents of the city of Pensacola were *passionate* about this project, whichever way they leaned.

I was thrilled to sell ads for this edition because I loved engaging in conversations about the project with business owners. I earned eighteen thousand dollars in commissions from that edition alone—almost as much as my yearly earnings—in just one month! That experience proved to me that if I'm excited about something, I'm much more likely to succeed at it.

A few months later, Ballet Pensacola, our city's renowned professional and academic ballet, announced that they were seeking a new executive director. And I, the fresh-out-of-college gal with little work experience, who was selling ads door to door, decided I was the one for the job. I sent in my resume and was called in for an interview. I was so nervous when I showed at their studios, but I was prepared to convince them that this job, one I knew I could be so passionate about (as a former dancer), was a perfect fit. I sat down, portfolio of work in hand, and prepared for questions from the board of directors. Their first question: "Who are your mom and dad, and what do they do?"

Perhaps I was naive. I wasn't expecting that question. I was prepared to share about my strengths, why I wanted the job, what I had done in hard situations, and more. My mom and dad? Why in the *world* were they asking me this?

"My mom is an elementary school teacher," I explained. "And my dad works for the power company."

"And their last names . . . ?"

Ohhh . . . I started to pick up on where this was headed. I was being asked if I brought any societal clout to the table.

"Cowan," I said boldly. "My mom is a beloved third-grade teacher at a magnet school with a focus on the arts. The best there is really. She loves her students dearly and taught me a lot about creativity and problem solving. She instilled a love of dance in me. My dad didn't graduate college or go to medical school, like he could have, because he was ready to settle down in a stable job, plant his roots in Pensacola near his parents, and start a family with my mom. He's the hardest working man I know."

They exchanged glances and kept going. I got that job. And then I went back to the not-always-kind magazine editor and resigned, explaining that I was leaving to take this role, to follow my love for the arts and my interest in fundraising.

She looked at me, dumbfounded. "I know five extremely qualified people who applied for that job and didn't get it. No offense, but why on earth did they hire you?"

"Because I'm the girl for the job," I said. And I left.

No, I didn't have a ton of experience or a wealthy family with a fancy last name or even a resume full of accomplishments. But I had grit, and I had ideas, and I was excited to do a good job at something I knew I could excel at. I learned over those few days a lot about my worth. I am who I say I am. I am who God says I am. I'm not who you want me to be, board president who wants me to fit a well-to-do mold. I'm not who you want me to be, managing editor who wants me to stay small.

No. Now watch me be the girl for this job.

Who do I say I am?

Who does God say I am?

_____   _____

_____   _____

_____   _____

_____   _____

_____   _____

_____   _____

I excelled at that job. And it was *hard*. I was young and I was female, two things *I* viewed as strengths but others saw as weaknesses. I was sometimes the only woman at a Rotary Club meeting and the only person under forty at some board meetings. But I stepped up to the plate. If I didn't feel confident, I made sure I gave a firm handshake, welcomed the new person to the room, and held eye contact during conversations. If I didn't feel included, I introduced myself to the people I wanted to meet, made friends with the person sitting alone, and asked to pull up a chair to an otherwise full table. I might not have been the most qualified, but I knew in my heart that I would excel, that I could bring creative ideas to the table, that I could cultivate a great culture between staff, instructors, dancers, and board members, and that I would work harder than anyone.

I also learned about integrity—how vital it is to have integrity as a leader *and* as a person. To be a woman of your word.

> Be a woman of your word.

WOMEN LIVING THEIR LIVES WELL

Years later, after working for a few different nonprofits, I stepped off the corporate ladder to pursue Simplified full time and eventually surrounded myself with a team of fantastic women. I knew I wanted to run my company differently. I wanted to cultivate inclusion, kindness, creativity, and a focus on caring for each other like family. I'd worked in both great and *terrible* corporate cultures, and I wanted to do something different.

I started Simplified with the belief that I was creating not just a pretty product company but a company that would empower, equip, and inspire busy women to live their lives well. And even when it was just me doing the work, I vowed to uphold "women living their lives well" as integral to our culture. My team grew slowly. First friends volunteered to help, and then I was finally able to pay one person less than part time, then two more at part time, then another full time. Today Simplified is made up of eight women—and we do things differently.

First, we say no to things that aren't "simplified"—having

> We say no to things that aren't "simplified" and yes to things that are innately who we are.

too many meetings, requiring people to clock in and clock out, and working too long and too hard to simply peddle a product. Second, we say yes to things that are innately who we are as a brand at our core: hiring the person's character and integrity first, then training them in the skills needed for the role; valuing family over work *always*; and allowing each person on our team a seat at every table, regardless of whether it's part of their "job description."

We value simplicity, creativity, humor, grace, and family. We also strongly believe in the entrepreneurial spirit: if you don't know how to do something, work at it until you do; if you want to make something happen, work at it until it does; if something's not working, don't be afraid to make a change quickly and confidently. We're scrappy. We're hard workers. And we love enormously. We love our customers, and we really love each other.

I once heard a speaker at a conference say, "My employees are not my friends. They're my staff. And we avoid drama by leaving our lives at home and not bringing them to the office." It was then that I vowed never to use the word *employee* again.

If my team doesn't bring their lives to work, to share about their kid's first day at school or the perfect fiddle-leaf fig they found at Home Depot, or the fact that they got a new puppy

HOW TO BE THE GIRL FOR THE JOB:

SPEAK WITH CONFIDENCE.

HOLD YOUR HEAD HIGH.

GIVE A FIRM HANDSHAKE.

LOOK OTHERS IN THE EYE.

USE PROPER GRAMMAR AND

PUNCTUATION IN EMAILS.

BE TIMELY.

ALWAYS BE GRATEFUL.

SEND THANK-YOU NOTES.

and took her outside in the snow and she tracked mud into the apartment, then I think something's wrong. I want to know the women I work with. I want to know what makes them tick, what makes them frustrated, and what gets them excited. I want to be able to tap into that quirky excitement that each of them has and help them utilize it to make awesomeness happen for our brand and our community.

I want to make sure they have their kid's birthday off (because you should totally be celebrating, not working) and that they know they're being thought of on the day they have to take their mom in for blood work. Work can wait. It can be done at night. It can be done on the weekend. Good work can be done before the kids wake up, during naptime, and even in the car on the ride home to visit family (not driving, of course). Good work is good work. Let's all rock our responsibilities, give our work our very best, slay our deadlines, and then PUT IT DOWN.

Do your work with gusto and excellence, but for good-ness' sake, *go live your life*. Give Simplified your all, and then go give your life your all too. Flexibility and the agency to work hard and still live well shouldn't be reserved just for the wealthy or the people at the top of the company org chart.

> Good work is good work.

I realize not all companies operate this way. In fact, I can think of very few that do. But I wonder if maybe Simplified could be part of a sea change. Could we start leading people not with power and a firm hand but with grace and a servant's heart? Could we value each other enough to love the human, not just the employee? Could we do business differently, expecting both high performance and the ability to disconnect and refuel and perhaps even move the needle on the bottom line? Could we love people better and change the world a little in the process? Even if you're not leading a team, could you approach your relationships with more grace and less of an expectation of perfection? Could we honor our human relationships as simply that: human and imperfect?

I tell my team to take two weeks off beginning before Christmas and ending after New Year's Day. I've been asked before why in the world we operate this way with January 1 being such a key date for brands based on the start of the calendar year. My answer is simple: we can prepare and plan for that date ahead of time. Modern technology has given us so many advantages in scheduling, automating, and working remotely. We call that time our "soft close." We're available and we put out fires, but otherwise, we're away, enjoying the holidays and our families and refueling before the new year.

We also operate in "summer mode" during June and July. Many of my teammates have children who are home during these months. Some of us travel and work remotely. I don't care where they're working from, as long as they're getting their jobs done with excellence and integrity. For us, it goes back to hiring the right people for the culture we've created. We batch-plan our work six months at a time with two marathon meetings—one in January and one in May. That way, everyone knows the tasks expected over the next six months and can plan accordingly. Due dates and tasks are visible to everyone, and communication is kept open via text message, phone calls, video calls, and email.

And, guys. It just *works*. Define the life you want, and *make it happen*. I started this business to have flexibility as a mom. When my eyes shift to *any prize other than that*, I know I'm off track. Instituting our holiday soft close and summer mode changed the game for our team. We feel more dedicated to our work, not less. We work harder to batch tasks and plan wisely. And we're excited to find new ways to innovate and create for our community, to inspire them to live their best lives too.

Quint Studer, author of many bestselling leadership books and the pioneer behind Pensacola's beautiful Community Maritime Park, says two things that I live by when it comes to leadership: "Employees want to believe their company has a meaningful purpose. They want to know that their own job is worthwhile. They want to make a difference. If all three of these conditions are accomplished, bottom-line results will follow." Yes, and amen.

Whether you are selling shoes or spearheading a startup, you'd better find your roots in something that matters, something with a meaningful purpose. Maybe the shoes you sell help people with foot pain or give them the support they need to go on walks with their kids, or maybe the shoes give people confidence to stand proud in a room full of people. Whatever you do, believe in it. Passion for purpose is contagious. And success in business follows passion.

Quint also says, "Culture outperforms strategy every time, and culture with strategy is unbeatable." I can't tell you how many times I've tried to be a "good manager of people" and created handbooks, policies, and frameworks for meetings. I've read dozens of business books, and none of them affected me as much as that simple statement. Whether you're managing people are not, the culture you create around yourself matters more than anything else you implement. Simplified's culture is not "Emily Ley running a planner business with eight employees." It's a team of nine friends doing life and work together to serve women who want to simplify their lives.

If we see that one of our teammates is struggling (maybe they're home with a new baby, learning a new rhythm, or they're overwhelmed with all they have to do for a big deadline), we step up. We've even been known to divvy up tasks to give someone a day off when she just needs a break. We provide eight weeks paid maternity leave, send little thank-you gifts after every launch, and operate with a forever open-door policy—allowing anyone to sit in on any meeting if they'd like to learn more about another side of the company.

We all help choose Simplified Planner covers, even if we're not designers or artists or involved in production. Why? Because buy-in matters, because inclusive culture matters. And because even though those conversations can get *super tense*

DEFINE THE LIFE YOU WANT TO HAVE, AND MAKE IT HAPPEN.

(guys, we have serious opinions on gingham versus watercolor flowers and coral versus true pink), each of us understands our customers and potential customers in a unique and different way, whether we're painting the flowers or answering the emails or managing the warehouse.

YOU'RE A LEADER TOO

I've just talked a lot about running a team and acting as a leader. But even if you don't have your own team or aren't managing others in your job, you're probably serving as a leader in some way—be it within your family, at church, in an entrepreneurial endeavor, at your workplace, on a committee of some sort, or even in a friend group. Honoring the entire person is so important if you want to see excellence from them in the form of results and production. Cultivate culture first, strategy second, and the rest will fall into place.

My hope is that we're seeing a shift in workplace values. More companies are adopting better policies and providing more support to their teams. But if we spearhead this idea of people over profits in our own circles of influence (and each of us, regardless of position or social media status or social status, has influence), we can inspire a shift in the culture at large.

Let us remember to never get so busy making a living that we forget to live a life, to have the courage to flip what we think we know on its head, and to question why we've always done things a certain way. That is where real change begins.

benediction

May you have the courage to ask yourself, *Could there be a better way?* May God light your path with brightness and clarity and deliver you to good people to serve. May you remember that excellence is not a term reserved for the workplace and that a life well lived is one where both sides are in ever-evolving harmony with each other, one ebbing while the other flows, and then reversing the cycle. May you know that you are in control of building the good life you were called to live.

reflection

How do you want to treat people on a daily basis
in a way that values them as whole people?

How do you want people to treat you?

How can you lead and teach people by example how you
want to be treated and how you intend to treat others?

10

SERVE WITH KINDNESS

No act of kindness, no matter how small, is ever wasted.

AESOP

Building a life you love is fantastic. But what if the life you love could also contribute to the world in an even better, bigger, and bolder way? There are so many "go get 'em" books out there about how to achieve your dreams and make big things happen, but what I find is missing in many of those messages is the ways in which your beautiful life could contribute to the bigger picture of God's kingdom. How can this life you love inspire others, help others, and serve others? We'll talk about legacy in the next chapter, but for now, I want to talk about doing all things with kindness by serving and loving others well.

This seems elementary right? Let's all be kind. Easier said than done sometimes though. We are all human, so although kindness may be our goal, each of us still occasionally experiences jealousy, grumpiness, sadness, hurt, a short temper, regret, and anger. But what if we cultivated a spirit of grace that we extended to those around us? In his bestselling book *Unoffendable*, Brant Hansen says "Anger is extraordinarily easy. It's our default setting. Love is very difficult. Love is a miracle."[18]

Have you ever been scrolling through Facebook, Instagram, or Twitter and come across a post by someone about politics, parenting, or some other hot topic that *immediately* raised your hackles? Perhaps in that moment you felt like you needed to engage, to prove a point, to set them straight. I know I have. Sitting behind keyboards makes us feel a little anonymous sometimes, a little braver than we would be if we were having a conversation at the grocery store.

But what if, instead of engaging, poised to tap out a pointed response, we stepped back? What if we simply chose to leave it alone? To walk away? Sometimes the kindest thing we can say is actually nothing at all. Brant Hansen says, "Choosing to be unoffendable, or relinquishing my right to anger, does not mean accepting injustice. It means *actively seeking justice, and loving mercy*, while walking humbly with God. And that means remembering I'm not Him. What a relief."[19]

Wow.

Remember that time you came at someone hot with anger, wildly offended, and the encounter changed their mind and made everything peaceful and better? Yeah, me neither. It just doesn't work. We rarely change people's minds by arguing with them—on the Internet or otherwise (and I'd argue that I'm not even sure we're supposed to be focusing so much on being right and changing people's minds). What if, instead of approaching each other ready to react, we aimed to proactively be unoffendable and to instead extend grace and kindness in place of reaction?

That person who left that snarky comment on your Instagram post? Delete it and move on. You're in control of your space. You're a grown woman. Remember, hurt people hurt people and humans are exactly that—human. It may hurt. A lot of crappy things have been said about and to me online. But it would accomplish nothing for me or for the people who said those things to get angry, to fuss, to spout back with a well-worded retort.

How about that person who bumped into you at the store and didn't even acknowledge their mistake? Take a breath. Perhaps they're in a hurry because they have a sick child at home. Or maybe they're just being a jerk. Either way, it's okay.

What about that article you read online that you *really* disagreed with? (Isn't it funny how ideas can be presented online, sources cited, or perhaps opinions from literally *anything in the universe, true or false*, and the comments section degrades into madness?) Instead of hurling insults and anger at each other, what if we instead took a breath and listened? That's it! Could we simply listen and choose to be unoffended?

All of this circles back to the idea that we don't always have to be on guard, ready to swoop in to our battle stations at a moment's notice. What an exhausting way to live. But that doesn't mean we can't hold strong beliefs! If you hold a certain belief, you can *do* things that actually move the needle on that issue, whatever it might be, instead of spending your time losing your temper online. Nothing is ever really accomplished that way. It just provides interesting, dramatic reading material for others to waste their time on (and also stirs up *other people's* anger).

I've found it very rewarding to walk away from heated conversations and put my time or money or whatever it is where my words would have been. Do you feel strongly about racial justice? Look for ways you can get active in your community. Do you have a heart for single moms? Volunteer to babysit or donate clothing, gift cards, and more. Is the health of our planet important to you? Then do something! Take your kids to volunteer at a recycling center. Do what you can where you are when it comes to what's important to you.

SERVANT HUMANS

During one of my first jobs in corporate America, I was given a book called *The Servant Leader.* The title itself intrigued young Emily because the two words seemed to contradict one another. As a leader, I wasn't called to serve, right? I was called to lead. Let's take this out of the context of being a leader for a minute. Let's consider being a *servant human* (in whatever work or activities make up your life). To serve others is to hold their needs in high regard.

Jesus, who did the most impactful work history has ever known, didn't do it from a pulpit or a mansion or even a fancy office. He did it in fields, on riverbanks, and at supper tables. He didn't choose the best of the best, those who looked and acted like Him, or those who were the best behaved to serve.

He chose the opposite—the oppressed, the marginalized, the sick and hurting . . . the sinners. He served, and He allowed His work to benefit others more than Himself. Jesus was the epitome of a servant leader—a servant human. He chose love and kindness when others may have wanted to make a religious or political point, change a person's behavior, or even turn their backs on the humans around them.

Our world is tough. It's a fallen world. Everyone has an opinion, and most people are easily offended. We draw lines in the sand—us and them. We deprive groups that don't look or believe or love like us basic human rights. We don't pay both genders or even all races equally. It's messy out there. And people are hurting, suffering, and starved for love, equality, and acceptance, and most of all, kindness. Maybe you're even experiencing some of this right now.

Kindness counts. Kindness is spread through that customer service email you send. Kindness is spread during that phone conversation. Kindness is spread through that favor you do, the extra little bit of effort or generosity you throw in, the way you let someone know you're thinking of them. Perhaps the most powerful thing you do in the world is the way you give others love freely, regardless of whether you think they've earned it *or will even appreciate it*. Actively love them anyway.

As you step out and build the life you love—as you mindfully and intentionally build, stone by stone, the life you love—you'll find countless opportunities to do this. Write a personal note with that order you mail out. Set yourself a reminder of the day

"In a world where you

can be anything . . .

be kind."

—*Anonymous*

your friend's dad passed away so you can send her a note to let her know you're thinking of her. Text that friend who has a doctor appointment today. Turn your little boy's bed down in the evening while he's brushing his teeth to provide a little bit of comfort when he comes into the room to go to bed. Ask how someone is doing in a work email instead of jumping straight to tasks. Make your husband's favorite lasagna tonight, just because you know he had a big meeting at work. While you're at it, love yourself a little extra too. Draw a warm bath and light a candle (why not?). Go to bed a little earlier. Set the coffee up for tomorrow morning so it's waiting for you in the early hours.

A little kindness and a little love can go a long way. We saw this specifically during the Coronavirus pandemic. We saw musicians singing on Instagram to lift the spirits of their followers, seamstresses sewing masks instead of their usual goods to help healthcare workers, and friends delivering baked goodies or fresh cut flowers to front doors to show neighbors they are loved.

• • •

I want you to do something. The next person you encounter after reading this chapter, be it your child, a coworker, or the lady taking your order at the deli, pay them a compliment, just because and without expectation or agenda. Give them a hearty thank you. Actively show the love you're made of in a way that may make them smile after you've gone, something they'll tuck in their pocket to be a bright spot in their day and in the days to come. Maybe they'll go and do the same. Imagine the virality of something like that.

What feelings of offense can I unsubscribe from?

benediction

May you know that love is an unconditional thing by its very nature. Remind yourself that it is not a well that will eventually run dry or a luxury that can only be afforded by some. It is free, never-ending, fully forgiving, and readily available. Not only that, it is the magic potion of life. The great elixir. Our God made palpable and tactical through your hands and through your words. What power you possess! What greatness your life will create in the world!

reflection

What is one random act of kindness you could do today, without much effort, to start the domino effect of kindness around you? Who do you need to thank? Name that person here. Before you go to the next question, make that call, give that hug, or send that text. Remember, building the life you love requires action.

In what arena are you often offended? Parenting? Politics? Religion? What would it look like to simply unsubscribe from the feelings of offense? To stand strong on your beliefs and actively work toward the good you believe in (rather than engaging in fruitless disputes)? What freedom would that give you?

KEEP YOUR EYES ON ETERNITY.

11

CHOOSE LEGACY

Our fingerprints don't fade from the lives we touch.

UNKNOWN

Do you ever think about the mark you're leaving on the world? How you'll be remembered and what stories will be told of you after you're gone from this world? That is legacy. The concept of legacy used to make me think of "some people," as if legacy is a thing that can be achieved only by those who make speeches on grand stages, write bestselling novels, or achieve some level of celebrity or success or notoriety. Yes, those people leave legacies, for sure. But legacy is simply the mark any individual leaves on the world around them, on their circles of influence, when they're gone.

The boldest among us choose to live life with a legacy mindset, that is to keep our eyes on eternity, not on the immediate future. Much like the "growth mindset" we discussed in the chapter on grit, those who have a "legacy mindset" aren't thrown off balance by the ups and downs of life because they understand the reality of their circumstances ebbing and flowing. They enjoy the ups, learn from the downs, and keep their eyes on the average upward trend—the way their opportunities, decisions, and offerings to the world keep them on that upward curve. It doesn't mean that it's not hard, just that what will bloom from your hard work (your toiling, if you will) will be beautiful in the end.

Your legacy is your life's work. And although we forget about it in the midst of busy Monday mornings and kids who don't want to go to bed and bills that need to be paid, it often *transcends* the day-to-day work you do in the world, the occupation that earns a paycheck for your family. Your actual legacy looks a lot more like the confidence and kindness you instill in your children, the character with which you interact with others, and the way you make those around you feel. Legacy isn't created in a vacuum or on an island. Rather, legacy is created by consistently choosing to uplift, to inspire, to give, and to serve.

> Legacy is created by consistently choosing to uplift, to inspire, to give, and to serve.

Think about some of the most powerful and lasting public legacies: Jesus Christ, Dr. Martin Luther King Jr., Maya Angelou, Mother Teresa, Ghandi. These people didn't come from wealth or have the privileges many of us have. They simply acted in love—they rose above the ins and outs of the day's work to engage in missions larger than any temporal earthly achievements. They did kingdom work because they believed in it: at supper tables, on city streets, and in villages.

CHOOSING LEGACY

A few weeks ago, I met a mother from a small town in Alabama. Candace is striking and gorgeous, a tall, beautiful Black woman with a warm smile and an unshakable spirit that exudes from her immediately. Candace is a single mother to teenage boys. When she was pregnant, with a toddler at home, the boys' father was tragically killed in a work accident at a manufacturing plant. Candace was beyond devastated. She recalls sitting on the hospital floor, holding her beloved's hand while she did all she knew to do and "prayed him into heaven." Candace explained to me how broken and alone she felt after this tragedy. Somehow, though, she knew she had to pick up the pieces to create a good life for her sons.

What struck me about Candace's story is that she told it with such conviction and grace. While grieving and healing from the aftermath of this horrible accident, she set her eyes on the eternal picture. Here she was, a mama to boys who needed her, who missed their father, and she had a choice: to allow their lives to fall apart in misery or to create a legacy in honor of their dad and in honor of the men she and her husband both hoped their boys would become.

Candace chose legacy.

She worked tirelessly to support her family. She made sacrifices. She worked long hours. But she's doing it. With pride, confidence, and strength found from her dedication to teaching her boys values that matter. Isn't it wild to think that in our darkest moments, when we think we can't possibly go on, strength is somehow born? That an eternal mindset can somehow survive or even be created from a deep loss like that? And beyond that, that the mindset can actually *thrive*? Those moments have the power to reveal what we really believe.

I asked Candace, having gone through this crisis, what she knows for sure about God. Without missing a beat, she said, "He always shows up, even when you aren't sure if He's there. He never forgot me and my boys."

Like Candace, I want to remember that daily pain and struggle is worth it—to build a legacy, to work for something larger and more beautiful than anything the world can throw at us. We get to choose our legacy and know that we aren't forgotten when we are doing kingdom work.

LEGACY MINDSET

I believe our legacy perspective sets Simplified apart from other planner companies and is part of the reason why we grew so quickly. Our mission is rooted in something meaningful, with a growth mindset, and is dedicated to serving others, not just selling to them. We are a business and we operate for a profit, but we do so because we believe we can improve women's lives. We don't just believe our planners are the best and prettiest out there; we believe that using them will *actually* improve people's lives. We offer a lot of purpose and value to our customers, beyond simply a stylish six-by-nine agenda.

Over the years, Simplified has dabbled in wholesale, eventually earning placement in more than eight hundred retail stores worldwide. We've been offered the opportunity to create lines of Happy Stripe kitchenware, baby goods, and women's clothing. We even made an app once that cost north of thirty thousand dollars and hundreds of hours of work (and headaches). Some of these were mistakes. All were learning experiences. But none of them, at least up until now, have aligned with our vision of growing "deep, not wide" (growing more intensely connected to what we're about rather than less connected by major growth) and staying truly committed to our goal of creating the simplest, most effective planning and organizational tools for busy women—and directly offering tools and educational materials to help them simplify their lives.

Sometimes the best way to build legacy is to *remove* a few kind-of-good ideas from your plate rather than adding another great idea, to allow the great one that's already there room to flourish. It's a lot like tending a garden—we weed and prune to allow what we care about most the space to grow. That can often feel counterproductive. Why would we cut something back when we're trying to allow it to get bigger and better? Well, sometimes parts of our dreams and visions actually hinder more than they help.

And the practice of identifying the dead weight, if you will, is a discipline that has served me *so very well*, not just at home, but in business as well. Make space for what matters most by tearing down a little of what you built. You may be surprised at how quickly

Evaluate your dreams and goals. In what ways can you take them deep not wide?

_____

_____

_____

_____

_____

blossoms begin to form on what remains. And once you've made space for that special thing, go after it with all your heart.

What work are you doing? Raising children full time? Teaching in a school? Styling hair? Selling tires? Whatever you do, "work at it with all your heart" (Colossians 3:23). Dig in the dirt, and find the roots beneath that product or service you provide. Make sure they're firm, healthy, and not overcrowded. Feed the roots. Love them. Why does what you do matter? Because it goes so far beyond the actual tasks to the way you interact with and serve others and leave margin for the life you love.

The poet Kahlil Gibran once said:

And what is it to work with love? It is to weave the cloth with threads drawn from your own heart, even as if your beloved were to wear that cloth. It is to build a house with affection, even as if your beloved were to dwell in that house. It is to sow seeds with tenderness and reap the harvest with joy, even as if your beloved were to eat the fruit. It is to charge all things you fashion with a breath of your own spirit. . . . Work is love made visible.[20]

• • •

I was named after my great-grandmother, Emily. I never met her. But I'm told she was strong, as warm as warm could be, and witty. She was a single mother in a time when that was frowned upon and took the bus to the makeup counter at a department store in Montgomery to provide for her only daughter. She never let her different family arrangement affect the fact that she wanted to provide a healthy, happy family and upbringing for her daughter, my grandmother. Though it was just the two of them until the time my grandmother married, my great-grandmother kept her eyes on what mattered. And her legacy lives on beyond her.

I polled Team Simplified on their individual definitions of *legacy* and put together the following collective list of ideas.

- What my children will tell their children about me.
- Making eternal decisions, not temporary ones.
- The lasting parts of life I get to create and celebrate—family, true friendships, hopefully an inspiring mindset.

- The impact of my actions. How I made people feel and how I poured into my kids and family.
- The parts of my life that people identify as important and good and faithful and they want to emulate for themselves.
- "Well done, good and faithful servant" (Matthew 25:21). Choosing to love when it was hard.
- That my life is a picture of God's love and a pursuit of God's purpose. I hope I will have finished the work He gave me to do and that other people's lives were impacted because of it.

Legacy is created *equally* in the grand gestures and in the monotony of repetitive tasks. In packing that lunchbox again and again. In buttoning little buttons with loving hands. In snuggling at bedtime just a minute longer. In kindly thanking the customer service representative on the phone. In making a warm meal after a long day again and again. In checking on an elderly neighbor who has no family to speak of. In listening when we'd rather speak up. And in speaking softly and with kindness when all patience has evaded us. It's in one more diaper changed. One more favor done. One more stranger helped. One more heart soothed.

YOUR GOOD LIFE

My dad (known affectionately as Pop Pop) is sixty-five. He is the oldest of five children and one of the greatest men on the planet. He's strong and kind and smart as a whip. Back in late

2019, he drove me to the airport. He talked to me about pandemics (little did he know what was coming) and World War I and parenting. That's what you get with Pop Pop: a mixed bag of genius and hard-won knowledge.

I say hard-won because my dad dropped out of college. He wanted to get married and was ready to commit to what amounted to a forty-year career with our local power company.

He could have been a doctor. He could have been a lot of things. He's that smart. He's the one we call when someone has a weird rash or when we aren't sure if we should call poison control because someone took a bite of a bar of soap (true story). He's brilliant and he's always right. But he wanted to be a husband and a dad and, eventually, a grandfather. He was often selected for but eventually turned down promotions that would have moved our family to Birmingham, Jacksonville, even Brazil.

His dream was to have a quiet life in the suburbs of Pensacola with my mom and close to his parents. He lost his dad last year and his mom years before that. I asked Dad if he regretted any of his decisions to support that "good life" he was after.

"Not for a minute," he said. "I wanted to be able to take you and your brother to the airport. To be there when my dad needed me toward the end of his days. To be the glue that kept our big family together." And so, for probably the tenth time in a year and a half (since we've moved back to Pensacola), he pulled my suitcase out of the back of his truck at 6:30 A.M., gave me a hug, and told me he'd see me at 10:00 A.M. on Wednesday to pick me up.

Sometimes good is really great.

What's your definition of legacy?

What's the good life you're after? Do you ever feel guilt or confusion about not wanting it to be more or about celebrating right where you are? I know I have in the past. The world makes us think we have to go after great and big and more. I hope my dad's story warms your heart and inspires you to do the little things that add up to grand moments and traditions that shape lives for generations to come. Legacy is made up of these things. I can only hope that all my work culminates in a legacy of love like this, with years of constant tending and consistent love and sacrifice.

Thanks for the ride, Dad.

What makes a good life?

What are the little things, the mundane things, that add up to a good life? How can you identify the beauty in each of them?

Every time I fold my kids' clothes, I can pray over where those clothes will take them each day.

Every time I send a good morning text to my mom adds up to a tradition of love.

Now list your own:

_____

_____

_____

_____

_____

_____

_____

_____

_____

_____

_____

_____

benediction

May you live a beautiful life that transcends your own body
and time on earth. May you reflect your Creator in every
big and small thing you do. And may you remember that
your legacy story is continually being written with each
ordinary day. Rise from the repetition of your work to see the
story being told, and allow your feet to be grounded in the
present, where we do the work that will shape the future.

reflection

What stories will one day be told about you?

What is the legacy you are building? Does it differ from what you
want your legacy to be? How so? How can you change that?

How might the sometimes-ordinary work of your days
spread love to the depths and breadth of the world?

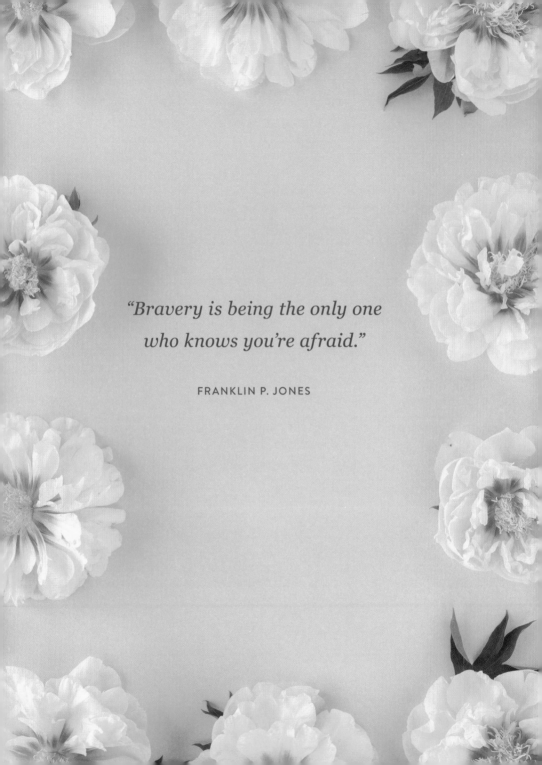

"*Bravery is being the only one who knows you're afraid.*"

FRANKLIN P. JONES

BUILD

Do what matters.
Forget the rest.

Part Five

I hope this book communicates a number of things to you. I hope it feels like you're sitting in my living room, cup of coffee or tea in hand, reflecting on who you are and who you want to be. My prayer is that these words feel like they're coming from a sister, someone who's been there, and is here to give you a hand and challenge you to look inward and onward.

Top among my prayer for this book is that you will see the power you have—right now, right where you are, with what you have. I want you to see that you have choices. And that with those small choices—brick-by-brick—you can build something you love. I hope you will see that your heavenly Father didn't make a single mistake when He created you but instead crafted into you a glorious, quirky, fantastic, colorful, multi-dimensional woman. Thank God we have *you* in this world!

It may not be easy to get where you want to go, but if you dare to do the work, cull the clutter, and to commit to the best, favorite, and necessary, that life you love can be yours. Be willing to discern the essential from the nonessential and to boldly and unapologetically care for your heart, body, and soul along the way. As Greg McKeown says, "You must protect the asset."[20] And you, my dear, are the asset.

12

FIGHT LIKE AN UNDERDOG

*You can choose courage, or you can choose
comfort. But you cannot choose both.*

BRENÉ BROWN

Successful people possess a certain scrappiness, a willingness to roll up their sleeves and do the work, to think outside the box, and to problem-solve with constant forward motion. This is also the mindset of an underdog: someone who is believed to be less than she actually is, who is predicted *not* to win. And this scrappiness is the secret sauce—to the success of Simplified and to the success of many others. Don't tell me what my limits are. Because while I may not be the most talented in the room, I am for sure the hardest worker.

You can't argue that. It's one of the things I know for sure about myself. I wish I was a formally trained graphic designer. I wish I'd gone to school to learn more about back-end business. But they don't teach scrappiness in those places. You learn to fight like an underdog only when you've been the underdog.

We decided a few things when we started my company:

1. We will run this company debt-free to protect our family and our employees.
2. We will grow deep, not wide, so that we can work to live, not live to work.
3. We will always value people over profit because that's what matters.

I was new to Tampa when I started this little venture. Because I was working full time at the University of South Florida, I could only carve out evenings and weekends to work on the business. And I had no idea what I was doing, so a lot of YouTube video–watching and Googling took place before actual work began.

Because I had recently relocated, I didn't have many friends, so I kind of adopted a few significant others from Bryan's friend group. We didn't have a ton in common, but our boyfriends or husbands were all work buddies, so it made sense.

They were smart, successful, and had been friends for a long time. And I was the new girl. With a side hustle.

Guys. It felt like middle school all over again—except I was twenty-five.

I felt like the joke. I knew of only two other friends at the time (back in Pensacola) who were trying to earn money with their creativity. One was a photographer for friends. The other made monogrammed T-shirts. At least in my sphere, starting

What are your nonnegotiables as you look at building *a life you love?*

I will . . .

_____

_____

_____

_____

I will . . .

_____

_____

_____

_____

I will . . .

_____

_____

_____

_____

your own business was something people just didn't seem to pursue as much back then. What I was doing seemed weird to some of my acquaintances. You either got a corporate job and climbed the ladder, or you were a stay-at-home mom. I wanted both—but with a twist. I wanted to work doing something that inspired me *and* to have flexibility for a family.

"Oh, that's cute . . ." they would say. I was excluded from get-togethers because I sometimes had to work. At other times, it seemed like they just thought I was weird, devoting so much effort to something so seemingly insignificant compared to their corporate careers, preferring to spend my free time learning how to use a printer rather than shopping at the local mall for handbags I couldn't afford. It felt like I got a lot of side-eye and some snickers when I'd share what I'd been up to or that I'd chosen to stay at home testing paper samples into the wee hours of the morning instead of barhopping at the trendy places downtown.

I pretended to be confident in these moments, but I was genuinely thirsty for real friends, especially friends I could share this new passion with, so I kept trying. But that confidence was all a front. I'd invite them over for girls' nights and host dinner parties so we could all get to know each other better, but inserting myself into a friend group that wasn't right for me never really got me anywhere.

I'll never forget going to a major league baseball game with that group of friends, approximately five other couples. At the end of the first inning, without saying a word, all the girls got up and moved to a nearby area of open seats, leaving me with the guys. I considered following them, but it seemed clear they were making a statement. I felt a lump rise in my throat as I awkwardly tried to find someone to talk to. Eventually I excused myself and "went to the bathroom."

Have you been there before? You excuse yourself to go to the bathroom or take a call, but really you're just trying to hold it together to keep people from seeing the hot tears welling uncontrollably in your eyes? For some reason, one of the girls followed me out and I unloaded on her, asking why they were acting that way toward me and explaining that I just wanted to be friends.

I have to hand it to her. At least she was honest with me. She told me I wasn't welcome, that they didn't understand me, and that I was just "different" from them.

I was shattered but not shocked. She was right. I wasn't welcome, they didn't understand me, and I was different from them. But mostly, I was lonely. As Bryan approached and she turned away, I felt a new clarity begin to form in my heart. We left the game, and I vowed to rise above this kind of nonsense. In my hurt that day, God reached out and blessed me to be able to see past those hurtful words and actions to the root of why people respond in these ways—their own pain or something else that had *little or nothing to do with you or me.* God put a firm resolve in my heart that day too—that I would fight for my dreams *and* be kind. Always.

You can say hurtful things to me. You can judge me for the goals I'm working toward. But I will not let you bring me down. I don't belong to you. And your opinion of me matters very little. Now watch me.

Watch me, I thought, standing outside that baseball game. *Watch me fight like the underdog.*

That's fine if you don't want me to sit with you, if you want to be a critic who doesn't understand what I'm doing. Your opinion doesn't affect me or my dreams. I'll build my own group, my own table, and fill it with humans who are kind. And here's the best part: I'll save you a seat for when you're ready to join us. Because I know that hurt people hurt people. And my table has a seat for everyone.

You may have heard or read this quote by Theodore Roosevelt, from a speech he gave in 1910.

> *It is not the critic who counts; not the man who points out how the strong man stumbles, or where the doer of deeds could have done them better. The credit belongs to the man who is actually in the arena, whose face is marred by dust and sweat and blood; who strives valiantly; who errs, who comes short again and again, because there is no effort without error and shortcoming; but who does actually strive to do the deeds; who knows great enthusiasms, the great devotions; who spends himself in a worthy cause; who at the best knows in the end the triumph of high achievement, and who at the worst, if he fails, at least fails while daring greatly.[22]*

When I first heard this quote in a TED talk from Brené Brown, something about the experiences all those years ago came into sharper focus. Though I didn't have the words for it at the time, my gut and God helped me identify what wasn't serving me, whose voices didn't matter, so I could pull myself above the fray and dig deeper into my dreams.

That friend group eventually fell apart. It happens. And sometimes it's for the best of everyone. I went on to seek new friendships in places that made more sense for me and count myself blessed to have a group full of girlfriends who lift each other up day in and day out. I hope those women from my past have found the same as well.

If you're in a valley—whether it's with friends, family, work, or something else—keep going. If you put one foot in front of the other, you'll eventually fight your way out to the top of the mountain, where you can see clearly what your next steps should be.

DON'T TELL ME WHAT I KNOW

"Don't tell me what I know, Travis!"

This funny line is from the Disney movie *Zootopia*. (I'm a mom. All truths eventually loop back to a Disney movie.) But this line really amps me up to fight like an underdog in so many ways. Bryan and I say it as a joke to each other about work and life, especially as it relates to our entrepreneurialism: "Don't tell me what I know!"

Over the years, advisers and business coaches have told Bryan and me that it was time to raise capital or take on investors. We even applied to *Shark Tank*, making it a few rounds into interviews but ultimately pulling out of auditions. It just didn't feel right to us.

Why? Because the world was saying we were supposed to do things a certain way, and we didn't subscribe to that. We were the underdogs—the entrepreneurs who had chosen not to take business loans to kickstart the company (opting instead to grow slow and smart), the go-getters who had decided to wear all the hats in the company (rather than hiring a team right off the bat), and the leaders who believed we were capable before we had evidence to support it. We may not have had all the money in the bank, all the skills in the toolbox, or even support from the people around us, but we believed we could make it with hard work, focus, and conviction.

> Underdogs are scrappy. Good underdogs are also full of integrity.

And we did. And we're not done.

To the ones who doubted, we said:

1. Don't tell me I have to go into debt to start or grow a company. If I put five dollars together over and over again, I'll eventually have a hundred dollars. Even slowly, the investment will grow.

2. Don't tell me I have to work a hundred hours a week for years on end to be successful. I know that if I work smart—and focus on the things that matter most—I can accomplish big goals.

3. Don't tell me I need a giant team to run a big company. If I hire the right people and we prioritize well, we can grow deep, not wide.

Underdogs are scrappy. Good underdogs are also full of integrity. The best underdogs give those coming up behind them up a boost. They pull up a chair for both the big dogs and the underdogs at their table. They make their circles and spaces better because of the goodness they bring to them through the fight.

You may not feel like you have everything you need to build the life you love, whatever that life might be. You may not have enough money, enough support, enough time, or enough resources. I challenge you to quiet your heart for a moment and question every single one of those reasons to seek out the glimmer of opportunity that lives on the other side. I know you're probably tired, overwhelmed, and unsure. But you're reading this book, which means *you have a dream.*

Be encouraged! I am proof that you can build something out of next to nothing, even if you feel ill-equipped, even if you're afraid, even if you feel alone or foolish at times. Yes, you can build a life you love. But you must *be bold enough* to do it. You have to look your challenges and excuses and your critics in the face and tell them to sit down. You may not be the most talented, you may not have the most money, you may not feel the most confident. But if you're the hardest worker in the room, nothing can stop you.

PS: I'm in your corner. Seriously. Even if everyone in your life is telling you you're crazy and that your dream is too big and too scary and too expensive and will take too long, you've got me! I was told all those things too. I sometimes even believed some of them. But if you've got enough spirit and fight in you, you've got what you need. Fight hard. Build the table of your dreams. Make space for everyone.

"The difference between a

successful person and others is

not a lack of strength,

not a lack of knowledge,

but rather a lack of will."

—*Vince Lombardi*

benediction

May you identify what you care about and what's
important to you . . . and go after it. May you commit
to your dream with all your heart. May you seek, find,
and fan the flames of the fire that lives inside you.
And as you fight for your hopes and dreams, may you
remember to always be kind. Kindness counts, always.

reflection

"Don't tell me what I know."
Tell me what you know about yourself
for sure, about who you are.

Are you the underdog sometimes?
How? How does it make you feel?

You may not have the most money, the most support, or the
most time, but you've got fight in you. We're watching.
How will you show up for your life?

13

PURSUE WHAT MAKES YOU COME ALIVE

You never know what you can do until you try.
And very few try unless they have to.

C. S. LEWIS

In high school, I auditioned and was chosen to be part of my school's color guard. At some schools, color guard was an extracurricular activity, something kids did just for fun. At Tate High School, however, color guard was life. It was fiercely competitive, backed by decades of world-class championship placements, extremely talented dancers, and a long history of excellence. Color guard is commonly referred to as the "sport of the arts," rooted in dance with the addition of flags, sabers, and mock rifles. Much like majorettes, we tossed and spun our equipment high into the sky before (hopefully) catching them and earning the applause of the Tate Chaparrals' many fans. I suffered countless bruises, a few wrist sprains, and more than one black eye. Once, a rifle hit me in the face so hard that my braces stuck to the inside of my mouth and had to be meticulously removed. But I digress.

It was hard. We practiced more than twenty-five hours each week on top of our studies. But we lived for winter guard. This was when our unit would put together one special routine, performed many times over the course of the season in a gymnasium, complete with costumes, music, and beautiful choreography. The way my body connected with the music, the way it felt to practice something over and over and over until near perfection . . . those four years of my life shaped my determined spirit.

My junior year, our director decided that our performance that winter would present the historical story of Jesus Christ. I went to a public school, where faith and academics did not intermingle, so this was a bold choice. But because our show was based on history and fact, not faith, it was allowed.

> The way my body connected with the music, the way it felt to practice something over and over and over until near perfection . . . those four years of my life shaped my determined spirit.

The show opened, not to music, but to a reading of the poem "One Solitary Life" by James Allen Francis. It was disarming and unbelievably moving. As this incredible poem was read, choreography set to the rhythm of the spoken words culminated in four girls performing the most difficult of skills: a "walking five" performed with a mock rifle. This is where the rifle is tossed into the air (while walking), spins five times, and then is caught steps from where it was originally released. It's so difficult to perfect. And *so* beautiful when perfected. I was chosen to be one of the four girls who would perform this part of the show. The end of the poem would boom over the loudspeakers:

All the armies that have ever marched
All the navies that have ever sailed
All the parliaments that have ever sat
All the kings that ever reigned put together
Have not affected the life of mankind on earth
As powerfully as this one solitary life.

The word *life* would be followed by ten seconds of silence. That word was also the cue for the four of us to begin the treacherous walking five. It was the moment the rifle should leave our hands, launch into the sky, do its thing, and be properly and perfectly caught. The snap that sounded when the rifles collectively hit our gloved hands cued the song that followed, "What Child Is This?"

It was beautiful—art and choreography coming together at its finest to tell a story that deserved nothing less than perfection. When performed perfectly the moment elicited roaring cheers and goosebumps. When performed incorrectly, well . . . when someone dropped their rifle or missed their catch, it was horrendously embarrassing. We performed this show for months. Some competitions we did better than others. But we worked up to the Winter Guard International World Championship in Dayton, Ohio, where world-class color guards from all around the world gather to compete. The days-long competition held many rounds, narrowing down to the few best color guards to compete in the finals.

This competition wasn't like any other competition though. We performed in the Dayton Flyers basketball arena (a far cry from the high school gyms we normally competed in). Not only was the arena enormous, but the ceiling was black.

Black.

Now, imagine you're tossing something high in the air, hoping to catch it perfectly, and the ceiling is *black*. The black ceiling always threw people off. And I just knew, deep down in my *soul*, that it would happen to me. The fear of dropping that rifle, in sheer silence, in front of thousands, the *crack* as it hit the floor, the devastation among my teammates at my one mistake . . . the pressure was thick and the fear lived with me all year.

During prelims, I was so scared of messing up that I was hardly able to enjoy myself out on the floor. I performed safely so as not to disappoint anyone. We scored well, but the performance didn't have the same power as it usually did. And apparently I wasn't the only one nervous. Everyone held back a bit.

Finals came along. As we stood backstage, the big moment upon us, layered in stage makeup, bouncing up and down to keep our muscles warm, wiping our hands dry, our instructor asked for our attention. "Before you go out there, I want you to remember the words of this poem, especially the very end. You weren't made to play safe or small. This is your one solitary life. You have worked all year for this very moment. Go out there and leave it all on the floor."

My fear mixed with adrenaline and the weight of what he was saying. *This is it. I can either go out there and play it safe, hold back, and have a decent performance and experience. Or I can give it all I have, right now in this moment, this one solitary life of mine. I can expend every ounce of energy and put to use every skill I was born with and have developed over years of hard, hard, hard work.*

The buzzer sounded that it was our time to take the floor. Rifles and sabers in hand, we high-fived one another and made our way out into the dim arena in front of thousands. We all took our positions and began. The poem started . . . and continued. All was going well. And then I heard . . .

"This."

My heart began racing.

"One."

You've got this.

"Solitary."

And . . .

"Life."

Go.

Up. Up. Up.

Snap.

Caught perfectly in my hands. I made an audible sound

of relief, and shock, and pride, and somehow, a photographer snapped my photo at the exact moment. The feeling I had inside was written all over my face. I have this photo in my house now, twenty years later, to remind me of the time when I nearly let fear pull me away from my calling, from an experience I would carry with me the rest of my life. What a gift it was to be able to pursue such a thing, to do something with four years of my life and with my body that made me feel *so very alive.*

My calling is not my vocation.

My calling, during those years, during that season, was to connect with that spark within me, that unique switch placed there by God, that would ignite my soul. What a miracle that I found it for a few brief years. And what an even greater miracle that I was able to leave all my fears on the floor that day and do a brave thing. I'll never forget the way that made me feel. And I've been chasing that *feeling of being most truly alive* ever since.

I know you've felt that spark. I know you know that feeling, even if it's somewhere deep, maybe hiding in your past. And everything we've been through together, through all the talk of goals and dreams, is just a way of going after that spark. Of building it into a life you love, day in and day out. When was the last time you felt that spark?

YOUR SPARK AND GOD'S CALLING

Our calling changes and evolves over the years as we grow and our circumstances change. My calling, during my high school

YOUR CALLING IS

TO CONNECT WITH THAT

SPARK WITHIN YOU,

THAT UNIQUE SWITCH

PLACED THERE BY GOD,

THAT WILL IGNITE YOUR SOUL.

years, was to connect with that spark, to develop a lifelong spirit of determination, and to learn grit, gumption, and scrappiness.

Those virtues served me well in my callings that followed—as a wife, mother, designer, and writer—as a friend, leader, and creator. The key to realizing your calling is to be comfortable with the fact that it will evolve as the seasons of your life change. So often, we believe our vocation has to be our calling, that the service we contribute to the world has to be deeply rooted in who we were made to be. I'd argue that that's not always the case. It's wonderful to pursue your calling as your career. But it's also okay to have a job that pays the bills and also have a calling that isn't required to fund your life.

Howard Thurman once said, "Don't ask yourself what the world needs. Ask yourself what makes you come alive, and go do that, because what the world needs is people who have come alive."[23]

Yes and amen.

There is inherent magic at the intersection of God's calling for our lives and what makes us feel truly alive. To discover God's calling for our lives, at least in this particular season, we have to know ourselves and know God. We do this by embracing who we are, celebrating what ignites our soul, and actively pursuing a relationship with God. If you travel the path toward what makes you feel most alive, and get to know God along the way, chances are you'll eventually find yourself at that magic intersection.

If you're at all like me, you might be thinking, *Emily, I want to know God. but where do I begin? I pray. I go to church. But I don't* know *if I really know Him or hear Him.* Tactically, here are a few ideas for communing with God on a deeper level:

1. **Pray simply.** Our prayers don't have to be fancy. In fact, they can be just a few words. I've found that repetition in prayer is sometimes really powerful—a trick I learned from Seth Haines, in his book *Coming Clean.* Seth struggled with alcohol addiction before getting (and staying) sober. When he would feel temptation wash over him, he'd step away and silently recite a simple prayer he learned from an old priest: "Lord Jesus Christ, Son of God, have mercy on me a sinner." It wasn't an elaborate or particularly beautiful prayer, but it was simple and full of grace. These few words, spoken to rebuke the temptations that stirred within him, became a rhythmic way he brought Jesus to the ring to help him fight, and it inevitably brought him closer to God.

> If you travel the path toward what makes you feel most alive, and get to know God along the way, chances are you'll eventually find yourself at that magic intersection.

When I feel fear creeping up—multiple times a day, sometimes multiple times an hour if I'm being honest—I will simply and silently pray, *Lord Jesus Christ, Son of God, have mercy on me a sinner.* There is beauty and power in simplicity.

2. **Read expectantly.** James 4:8 says, "Draw near to God, and he will draw near to you" (ESV). I sometimes struggle with this. I open my Bible, not sure where to start, and begin reading passages that I'm not entirely sure I understand. I've prayed hopeful prayers for God to help me connect with His Word. But in those times, I realized I was simply checking a box—reading my Bible because I thought it was a thing I should probably be doing, going in without expectation, and leaving empty-handed. It was only when I began to read *expectantly*, through guided readings and during group studies, that I began to draw nearer. I asked God hard questions. I confessed sins to Him. I even got angry about the twists and turns of my life. He met my expectancy with relevance, rich in both fact and faith.

> Lord Jesus Christ, Son of God, have mercy on me a sinner.

3. **Step boldy out of your comfort zone.** We can pray and read all we want, but if we're not acting as the hands and

feet of Jesus, communing with the lost, the broken, the marginalized, and the excluded, what are we really doing? Understanding God's way means loving and serving *all* people well, even those who may look, love, or believe differently than we do. If we always do what we've always done, we'll always be who we've always been. How boring. I guarantee this is one of the most fantastic ways to find that intersection of who you are and who God called you to be. Bring more people into your tribe. Challenge yourself to love better and to serve the way Jesus did—without fanfare, without exception, with open arms. We can discover so much about God's calling for our lives when we stop doing what we've always done, step outside our comfort zones, and allow ourselves to learn, to be challenged, and to discover that fire within us.

benediction

May you go forward with the bravery to fall short and try again. May you go forward expectant for God to make His calling for you known. The path to becoming the woman God called you to be is right alongside the path toward the woman you know you can be. There will be bumps, potholes, and puddles. For the world's sake, may you be willing to get dirty and to become truly alive.

reflection

The world desperately needs you to come alive. To be joyful and passionate and fully awake. In this process, what are the things you've recalled that make you come alive?

How does it feel for you to be fully awake, fully present, fully alive?

This is your one solitary life. What will you do (what matters) and what will you forget (the rest)?

14

DIG IN

The greatest gift you can give another is the purity of your attention.

RICHARD MOSS

Having written this book before COVID-19, I keep revisiting the last moments I have with you here. I want to hug you, to pull you near and tell you that brighter days are ahead of whatever difficult season you've gone or are going through. I also want to jump up and down and clap my hands, my ponytail waving furiously with my excitement, and yell, "YOU'VE GOT THIS! LET'S GO! I'm here, cheering you on!"

And also, I want to make you a cup of tea and invite you over for cookies and offer you a blanket when you walk in. Come curl up and let's talk about why this stuff is so important. Why we, as women, must not back down when life gets hard. Yes, we can cry and let the pain wash over us, but at the end of the day, we must never agree to settle for mediocrity.

We've each been given a sacred gift: a number of days to spend here on this earth with our people. And I want to leave you with a challenge: work your tail off. Hustle like mad. Get after it, whatever *it* is to you.

And then, for the love of all things holy, rest.

Take care of yourself. Treasure your heart, mind, and body the way God treasures you. And then . . . get up and do it again. We will never regret this life if we leave it all on the court. I hope I am absolutely used up at the end of my days—having given every ounce of love until I had no more left to give, having pursued every curiosity big and small, frivolous or meaningful, and having fully blossomed and poured every ounce of Emily out onto the world so other flowers can come up behind me.

That's the key. You are not alone. You have sisters, women who are different from you, similar to you, and believing with you that growing is one thing but growing *boldly* is quite another. Thank You, God, for sisters—both biological and chosen.

Could it be that caring for ourselves and each other (much like tending a flower in a garden) actually helps the entire garden to grow in unison? When we flourish, does that open the door for others to flourish as well? And what if that sparks a chain reaction that makes each of us better?

SOUL CARE

So what *is* soul care and how does it come into play when you're hustling to make something happen? To build a life you love?

I'd like to argue that soul care is the secret to achieving the ever-elusive holy grail that is "balance." For every action we must counteract it with an equal yet opposite reaction. We must roll up our sleeves and do hard work . . . and then make a space for rest. We must give of our time and resources for the well-being of others . . . and then turn our efforts inward, to strengthen, heal, and fuel ourselves.

Some people might say this is selfish. But I'd argue that it's actually selfless. To truly care for your calling—for the life you are building, for the family you're creating, for the dream you're pursuing—you have to be willing to do the hard stuff, to stay up late and sacrifice, and to hustle. And you have to be *equally* willing to make the difficult decision to let certain efforts wilt away—to choose the kids' Valentine's Day party at school over the conference call, for example—and to actively pursue rest and refueling as much as you pursue achievement and success.

You lean in. You listen to the desires of your heart.

Sit back and listen. Don't try to change them. Identify those desires and feed them. If your soul comes alive when you write, put pen to paper. If your soul comes alive when you dance, turn up the music. If your soul comes alive when you sing, even if off-key, sing it out, sister.

Feed your soul what *makes it come alive.* Set boundaries to protect what matters. Know your value and make yourself a priority. Listen to your body when it needs rest or movement or nourishment. Recognize and acknowledge your heart of hearts. Here are some of the things I remind myself of regularly:

- You are building this life so you can have flexibility as a mom.
- You are building this life so that you can change the lives of women everywhere.

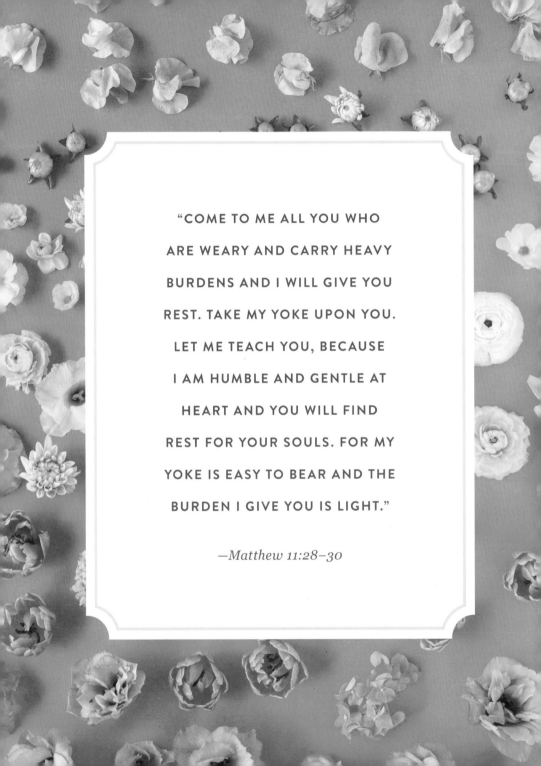

"COME TO ME ALL YOU WHO
ARE WEARY AND CARRY HEAVY
BURDENS AND I WILL GIVE YOU
REST. TAKE MY YOKE UPON YOU.
LET ME TEACH YOU, BECAUSE
I AM HUMBLE AND GENTLE AT
HEART AND YOU WILL FIND
REST FOR YOUR SOULS. FOR MY
YOKE IS EASY TO BEAR AND THE
BURDEN I GIVE YOU IS LIGHT."

—*Matthew 11:28–30*

- You are building this life so that you can leave a legacy of compassion and inclusion for your family.
- You will not sacrifice your soul on the altar of getting ahead. Rather, you will honor humans above hustle and a life well lived above a life well achieved.

SIMPLICITY RULES

The simplest ways to care for your soul involve getting back to basics, stripping away the excess and honoring the beauty found in order, simplicity, and focus. This is where things come full circle. I created Simplified because I was overwhelmed, and I return to those principles again and again.

Dare I say that simplicity is integral to the journey and paramount in the results of our hard work? When we address clutter in our lives—be it *tactically* in our cabinets, in our desk drawers, or even on our computer desktops or *figuratively* on our calendars, in our worries, or within our hearts—we make space for our souls to breathe.

Emily P. Freeman is an author and podcaster who has made this pursuit her mission: making space for her soul to breathe. I have put this phrase in my back pocket, as the underscore of why simplicity matters—not just as we seek to create beautiful pantries and picturesque junk drawers but as we move to eliminate the extra, the unnecessary, and the excess. Through these efforts, we hold space for something more valuable.

I was going through a hard time about a year ago—bogged

The desires of my heart:

_____

_____

_____

_____

_____

_____

_____

_____

A life well lived means for me:

_____

_____

_____

_____

_____

_____

_____

_____

_____

down by the weight of work and raising three kids and living in a new city—when a friend said to me, "I don't know how to fix it, Emily, but I'm going to sit right here and hold space for you."

I didn't know what she meant at first and had to think through her words. And then it clicked. She couldn't clear my clutter or fix my problems or care for my soul *for* me. Instead, she *could* sit and hold space for me. She could make a space for my soul to breathe, space to listen while I unpacked my thoughts and feelings. Space to be a friend when I needed communion. And space to reflect back to me the goodness I was struggling to see in myself.

What a beautiful way to care for each other, to allow each other to heal and grow, by making space.

But it's difficult to hold space for yourself or the people you love if your life is cluttered. Clutter is the enemy of clarity. When our lives are cluttered, whether it's physical, intellectual, emotional, or otherwise, that clutter edges out any space we need in order to process. And that space is what we need to gain clarity, to achieve our goals or the space to get clear on what they even are.

And this is the beauty of the BUILD concept—from beginning to end. Underpinning all the hard work and hustle it takes to build a life you love is this nonnegotiable: you *must* make space for your soul so clarity can manifest itself. This is true at the beginning of your journey, throughout the middle, and when you've reached the pinnacle of where you want to go.

CLARITY AMID CHAOS

The experiences that the entire world has gone through during a global pandemic have shaken me. Beyond feeling overwhelmed by what is happening, I feel a renewed urgency and intense yearning to live the life I've been given *fully alive.*

To live my life to its absolute fullest with however many days I'm gifted on this earth.

To love enormously and with abandon.

To be overwhelmingly kind and thoughtful.

And to shape my life to be the one I will have no regrets over at the end of my days.

The time our family spent quarantined shook my priorities into new levels of clarity and made me more certain than ever that growing boldly—not just as a single bloom but a colorful, wild, crazy garden full of uniqueness—is what we're all meant to do.

May we come together with the common goal of growing into the very best versions of ourselves we possibly can. What a glorious, beautiful image that brings up for me—each of us our own wild and colorful flowers, reaching toward the sun, intertwined with one another and bringing so much beauty to the world.

I could go on and on, but my curiosity toward flowers tells me that maybe it's time to get a pot and plant some seeds. I'll water them and see what happens. I hope you'll go nurture your curiosity too.

The world needs who you're growing to become.

benediction

May you have the drive and fortitude to roll up your sleeves, break
a sweat, and sacrifice when the time is right. And may you have
the gumption and bravery to clear the clutter in your life to make
space for the goodness that is sure to follow hard work. May you
honor your seasons—those that ask for hustle and sacrifice and
those that require your focused, quiet attention—creating lap
space for a young child, devoting focus to creating a new home,
or allowing your soul to heal, rest, and recover. Hold each season
beloved, as it will surely fade into another. Above all, may you fill
your soul with truth and His promises every step of the way.

reflection

You have one life here on this earth. How
will you spend the rest of it?

No more playing small.
Who is the woman inside you desperate to be released?

As we grow together, how will you balance hustle
with care for the heart of who you are?

JOY IS FOUND ALONG THE

BUMPY, BEAUTIFUL,

BROKEN YELLOW-BRICK

ROAD—WITH

EVERY IMPERFECT

CHARACTER WE MEET,

WITH EVERY WAY WE GROW

ALONG THE PATH,

AND WITH EVERY BATTLE WE

FIGHT THROUGH,

FLYING MONKEYS

OR NOT.

Chase Your Rainbow

watched *Judy* on a plane recently. It's the story of Judy Garland, played by Renée Zellweger. Undeniably talented, Judy Garland rose through the ranks of stardom in the 1930s, arguably most well known for her portrayal of Dorothy in the original *The Wizard of Oz*. Judy struggled with many ups and downs throughout her life, but the film culminated with one profound and beautiful statement at the very end that I believe shines a light on building a life you love.

Judy explains that one wonderful song embodies the hope she has for the future: *somewhere over the rainbow.* "It's a place of hope," she explains. And we are walking toward that magical place of hope together. She explains that the joy was found in the journey if she allowed "the walking to be enough."

Our greatest joy isn't found at the top of the mountain or even behind the gates of Oz. Rather, joy is found along the bumpy, beautiful, broken yellow-brick road—with every imperfect character we meet, with every way we grow along the path, and with every battle we fight through, flying monkeys or not.

I find it fascinating that this movie came across my screen on that particular flight, as I was finishing the initial draft for this book. It was oddly perfect timing for the girl who started with a little dream about a rainbow planner, the unshakable belief that she could build a life she loved, and the gumption to dare to do it.

I'd like to leave you with a letter, a note from me. A girl, who has faced more and less and different than you have in your life. Whose upbringing was different. Who may look or love or believe differently than you. I'm in your corner, cheering you on as you build a life you love.

Dear you,

You are different. You are different than you once were. You are different than the girl next to you. You are different than me. You are wild and unique and gloriously perfect in all those things. God delights in you. How fantastic to have a Father who absolutely adores you.

All those things that you think make you weird? Those are the traits that make you special! Identify them. Lean in to them. Grow boldly into the woman God is inviting you to be. Believe in who (and whose) you are. Imagine that life you dream of. Love all people well. And do what matters; forget the rest. Whether you are building a company, a family, a side hustle, a marriage, a mission, or a home—do the work. And honor the rest.

This is the magic of balance. This is the magic of building a life you love: honoring the ups and the downs, the work and the rest, the gains and the losses. And above all, allowing the walk to be enough.

Somewhere over the rainbow skies are blue
And the dreams that you dare to
dream really do come true

Chase your rainbow. Enjoy the imperfect journey. Dare to build a life you love.

Always in your corner,

Emily

ACKNOWLEDGMENTS

Bryan, you believed I could grow boldly before I did. Thank you for always being in my corner. I love you back.

Brady, Tyler, and Caroline, may you never ever doubt the grit you have inside. You can build lives you love, and your daddy and I will be there in the front row to cheer you on and help you up every step of the imperfect way.

Mom and Dad, thank you for instilling these virtues in me from the very start. My strength is a direct result of your love through achievements, mistakes, joys, and tears.

To all the women who allowed me to share their stories in this book, your bravery and gumption are the sparks inside these pages. You have bared your souls and will touch many. Thank you for sharing your journeys.

Team Simplified, I don't know how my path serendipitously crossed with each of yours, but it was surely the result of divine intervention. Thank you for listening to these words, chewing on them with me, and walking through each chapter of this book and each day of our mission as a team. I love each of you like family.

To my entire publishing team, I'm pretty sure I'm the luckiest author on the planet to be able to make good books with you. Thank you for believing in me to write this one with fire when I didn't first see the spark.

NOTES

1. William Saroyan, *The Daring Young Man on the Flying Trapeze* (New York: Modern Age Books, 1934), 12–13.
2. Mary Oliver, "The Summer Day," in *Poetry 180: A Poem a Day for American High Schools*, https://bit.ly/3dcOUTr.
3. Robert Morgan, Rule #2, in *The Red Sea Rules* (Nashville: Thomas Nelson, 2001).
4. As quoted in Eleanor Hooks PhD, *A Daily Sip of Joy and Peace* (Bloomington, IN: Balboa Press, 2016), 39.
5. Enneagram Type Two, The Supportive Advisor, https://bit.ly/36Lb26l.
6. As heard in teaching.
7. "The Top 20 Things Oprah Knows for Sure," *Oprah.com*, https://bit.ly/3iHBYGf.
8. Squire Bill Widener, quoted by Theodore Roosevelt in *Theodore Roosevelt: An Autobiography* (New York: Charles Scribner's Sons, 1913; 1920), 337.
9. Angela Duckworth, *Grit: the Power of Passion and Perseverance* (New York: Scribner, 2016).
10. Ibid., 34.
11. Shana Lebowitz, "A UPenn psychologist uses the 'Hard Thing Rule' to teach her kids to take control of their success," *Business Insider*, May 8, 2016, https://bit.ly/3iOD0QN.
12. Martin Luther King Jr., "Keep Moving from This Mountain" (address at Spelman College, Atlanta, GA: May 1, 1960), https://stanford.io/3nxU2q9.

13. David McClelland, quoted in Maarten van Doorn, "You Are the Average of the Five People You Spend the Most Time With," *Medium*, June 20, 2018, https://bit.ly/2SGhYcQ.
14. Jim Collins, "BHAG," https://bit.ly/33L57w1.
15. Robert R. Gilruth, "I Believe We Should Go to the Moon," *Apollo Expeditions to the Moon*, history.nasa.gov, https://go.nasa.gov/2SC5q6a.
16. Brené Brown, *Dare to Lead* (New York: Random House), 101.
17. Max Weigand, "Because of 4am: Inside the Mind of Kobe Bryant," *Medium*, November 8, 2017, https://bit.ly/3jXMvil.
18. Brant Hansen, *Unoffendable* (Nashville: W Publishing Group, 2015), 7.
19. Ibid., 104.
20. Kahlil Gibran, "On Work," in *The Prophet* (New York: Knopf, 1923), Poets.org, https://bit.ly/34G9Uyb.
21. Greg McKeown, *Essentialism* (New York: Random House, 2014), 91.
22. Theodore Roosevelt, "Citizenship in a Republic" (speech at Sorbonne, Paris, France, April 23, 1910).
23. Howard Thurman, as quoted in Gil Bailie, *Violence Unveiled* (New York: Crossroads, 1995).